# REFLECTION ON BERGSON'S PHILOSOPHY

A. Appan Ramanujam

SHARADA

**Sharada Publishing House**

Delhi

2008

*First Published: 2008*


ISBN : 978-81-88934-49-2



*Published by:*
Anjana Bansal
SHARADA PUBLISHING HOUSE
(Publishers on India's Past and Present)
111, Vidya Vihar Apartment,
Sector-9, Rohini, Delhi-110 085
Ph. : +91-11-3292 1560 (O), 2755 2102 (R)
E-mail: bansal_sph@rediffmail.com

*Printed at:*
Salasar Imaging Systems
Delhi

*Dedicated*
*to*
*My Parents*
*Smt. & Shri S. Alagar Ramanujam Ayya*

# Contents

# Acknowledgements

My humble endeavour in preparing and presenting this work would remain incomplete without sincerely acknowledging my deep sense of gratitude to my learned teachers Dr. S.P. Adinarayan, Thiru C. Ramalingam, Dr. V. Rathinasabhapathy, Dr. R. Kolappa Pillai and Dr. N. Jayashanmukham, Department of Philosophy, Annamalai University. I deem it a special privilege to learn under their erudite guidance and I must confess that they have given me the benefit of their deep insight and unstinted moral support and strength all throughout. I have no words to say how deeply conscious I am of their affectionate suggestions and able guidance.

My heartful thanks also go to Dr. E.I. Warrier, Professor and Head of the Department of Philosophy, Calicut University and Dr. Pete A.Y. Gunter, Chairman, Department of Philosophy, North Texas State University, Denton, Texas (U.S.A.) for their fruitful hints. I am extremely grateful to Professor Gunter for sending me his valuable suggestions and reprints of articles on the recent development of Bergson's Philosophy.

I must acknowledge the encouragement I received from my wife Mrs. Padmaleela and daughters A.R. Shloka and A.R. Prajna in completing this work. My thanks are also due to Dr. J. Rangasamy, Professor of Philosophy, Tamil University, Thanjavur for his keen interest in bringing out this volume. I am also grateful to Sharada Publishing House, New Delhi for publishing this work with perfection.

Finally, I offer my devotional gratitude to my devoted parents without whose unfailing affection, encouragement and inspiration during moments of depression, I could not have carried on this work to its completion.

Chennai
5-10-07

**A. Appan Ramanujam**

## Chapter I

# Introduction

Henri Bergson was a popular philosopher in the beginning of the twentieth century. He had a considerable effect upon French thought. He also influenced many thinkers of the West. Particularly his irrationalism made a wide appeal.

In recent times, there has been considerable development in Bergson's philosophy. Books and articles on Bergson continue to appear, both in France and the United States and also in Latin America. Recent interpretations of Bergson's philosophy show that his thought is relevant to the philosophy of science and has not received the careful and serious consideration in this respect that it deserves. The most famous exponents of the above view are Pete A.Y. Gunter and Milic Capek of the U.S.A. Gunter's *'Bergson and the Evolution of Physics'* and Milic Capek's *'Bergson and Modern Physics'* have brought about a revolution in the development of Bergson's Philosophy. Both these thinkers also hold that anti-intellectual interpretations of Bergson entirely miss the mark. Gunter is of the opinion that Bergson's philosophy contains a dialectical element which resembles Hegel's and Schelling's philosophies. It is this dialectic which unites the Bergsonian opposites : intuition-intellect, philosophy-science, memory-matter, life-entropy and the open—the closed society.

Apart from the above developments in Bergson's philosophy there are also areas in the development of Bergson's thought which have so far not been studied in depth : 1. The significant shift in Bergson's thought between *'Time and Free Will'* and *'Matter and Memory'*. 2. The shift which occurred between *'Creative Evpolution'* and *'The two Sources of Morality and Religion.'* 3. The change which can be noted between his *'Introduction to Metaphysics'* and the two 'Introductions' in *'The Creative Mind.'* Between *'Time and Free Will'* and *'Matter and Momory'* Bergson significantly changed his conception of external world, *away* from an almost Cartesian position. In the 'Introductions' Bergson reveals himself as almost a positivist, insisting very strongly on scientific knowledge as a base for philosophy and, inversely, insisting that intuition *must* be capable of verification on the scientific side. (To say this is by *no* means to make Bergson into a mechanist, a materialist, a behaviorist, etc.). Since Bergson is a seminal thinks his views on "The Two Source" and "Dynamic Religion" are relevant to Post-Modenism and Globalisation. The existentialists like Sartre had overshadowed Bergson's popularity in France.

The present work largely aims at a study of the shift of Bergson's thought that seems to have occurred between his *'Creative Evolution'* (1907) and *'The two Sources of Morality and Religion'* (1932). To compare the works of two philosophers is one thing and to compare the two works of the same philosopher is another. The first kind of comparative study is quite common because there is scope to enumerate similarities or dissimilarities between any two philosophers. Whereas in the second case such a study is quite uncommon because almost all philosophers normally do not change their standpoint. But Bergson does change his views in his later works. We notice that there is a significant change between 1907 and 1932 in his thought. Our aim in this work, therefore, is to inquire this change in opinions of Bergson.

The following is the brief account of the chapterwise discussion of this work :

A study in the development of a philosopher's views includes his background also. So in the first chapter Bergson's philosophical background is discussed : *i.e.,* his roots for his views on duration (duree), intuition, psychology, élan vital and morality and religion.

In the second chapter Bergson's concept of Reality (God) as enunciated by him both in his *Creative Evolution* (1907) and *The two Sources of Morality and Religion* (1932) are discussed. For Bergson, Change is the only Reality and Élan Vital is the dynamic force which acts from the *back of all species.* In the *Two Sources of Morality and Religion,* he jumps to a completely different view attributing Love and Creation to the Reality. Thus, the *impersonal* and the *indetermined* push of *Creative Evolution* becomes *personal and purposive* in his last work.

The third chapter deals with Bergson's metaphysics in which his views on intellect and intuition according to his earlier works (*Introduction to Metaphysics* and *The Creative Evolution)* are analysed. Here, Bergson talks of intellect and intuition only in the epistemological sense. Both intellect and intuition are the ways of knowing the Reality.

In the fourth chapter we see how the epistemological intellect of Bergson's earlier works is being *applied* to the moral and religious spheres. According to him there are two kinds of morality : 1. the closed and 2. the open. These two, though they are different are not mutually exclusive. In fact the closed morality always leads to the open morality. The first kind of morality is the offshoot of the intellect. As there are two kinds of morality, there are also two kinds of religion : 1. the static and 2. the dynamic. Under the topic of static religion, Bergson gives an account of the primitive religion, myth-making, magic, totemism, spirits, gods, sacrifice, prayer etc. Static religion is defined by him as 'a defensive reaction of nature against what might be depressing for the individual, and dissolvent for society, in the exercise of intelligence'. Here we must note that the static religion itself is a product of intelligence. Nature acts in such a way that intelligence is countered by intelligence itself.

In the sixth chapter we see Bergson as a mystic. Here, he speaks of two kinds of mysticism : 1. the complete and 2. the incomplete. According to him the Christism mysticism belongs to the former type because it is *active.* The Oriental and the Greek mysticism are of the latter type because they are only *contemplative* renouncing *social action.* The important point to be noted here is that the intuition which is discussed by Bergson only as a way of knowing in his earlier works becomes mysticism.

In the seventh chapter Bergson's shift in thought between his *Creative Evolution* (1907) and *The two Sources of Morality and Religion* (1932) is analysed. In the eighth chapter an attempt is made to relate Bergson's thought to Philosophy of Science, Post-Modernism and Globalisation.

As a result of our probing we have maintained that :

1. The Vital impulse (of Creative Evolution) gets identified with Divine Love and God in *The two Sources of Morality and Religion.*
2. The epistemological intellect of *Creative Evolution* finds application in the moral and religious spheres in *The two Sources.*
3. The sourceless and the endless Élan Vital of *Creative Evolution* finds source and end in the *Two Sources.*
4. Bergson admits Teleology in *The two Sources of Morality and Religion* whereas he vehemently opposes any kind of Mechanism or Finalism in *The Creative Evolution.*
5. Epistomological Intuition becomes Mysticism in his last work.
6. Intuition in *The two Sources* is a *rare-essence, practical and purposive.*
7. Shift in Bergson's thought is noticed in *The two Sources* with regard to the Roman Catholic Church.
8. Bergson's thought is relevant to Philosophy of Science, Post-Modernism and Globalisation.

## *Chapter II*

# Philosophical Background of Bergson

As Henri Bergson became the most famous philosopher in the world, he was welcomed. William James praised him on the publication of *Creative Evolution* : 'O my Bergson, you are a magician, and your book is a marvel, a real wonder in the history of philosophy, making, if mistake not, an entirely different era in respect of matter...... There is so must that is absolutely new that it will take a long time for your contemporaries to assimilate it'.[1]

But some were sceptical about his originality. Some others sounded a note of warning voice stating that Bergson's is a siren mysticism of which we must beware. One critic accused him of refusing to acknowledge his debt to Guyauk, Ward, and to William James.[2] Another critic believed that his thought stemmed from Kant and a few later French philosophers.[3] A Frenchman and a German both argued that Bergson's descent from Schelling and Novalis was evident.[4] Albert Kann finally wrote in anger that Bergson had plagiarised *The two Sources of Morality and Religion* from his (Albert Kann's) books which he had published many years earlier.[5]

In fact none of these views on the novelty of Bergsonism, whether favourable or unfavourable has been sufficiently justified. Taproots of Bergsonism have grown from the nourishing Hellenic soil, and others from the strata of the Middle Ages. Even the German romantic philosophers exerted their influence on Bergson through the agency of Frenchmen. However, we shall limit ourselves to the immediate scientific and philosophic environs of Bergsonism. *We can analyse on the five broad-cut facets of his thought* : 1. *His view of 'duration'*, 2. *His theory of intuition, his psychology, His élan vital* and *His morality and religion.*

## 1. BERGSON'S BACKGROUND FOR HIS VIEW OF 'DURATION'

Henri Bergson was one day taking his usual walk after lecturing at the lycee. He was troubled. He had been explaining the paradoxes of Zeno. They had no clear flaw. So, while he meditated, there struggled into consciousness a luminous point of thought. It was the idea of *duree,* which came to him long before its companion idea of intuition[6] ......'The object of my first meditations was to define the notion of time, which seemed incomplete and lacunary to me. And since then I have simply worked. I have worked with all my strength, without interruptions, without being obliged to change the rigorous method I have imposed on myself since the beginning..... Traditional philosophy is always systematic. I have wanted to create a different kind. By no means have I an answer to everything. I do not know to what conclusions my premises are going to lead. I have constant recourse to scientific documentation, and it is certain that my previous mathematical studies have been a great help to me'.[7]

**Herbert Spencer's Influence on Bergson :** Jules Tannery, in 1875 could sharply criticise the belief that sensations can be represented by mathematical symbols.[8] By this time Jules Lachelier argued that all causality is subordinate to purpose, and therefore to contingency; Bergson called Lachelier his teacher.[9] Boutroux, another teacher of Bergson also through his book *The Contingency of the Laws of Nature influenced Bergson*. The origin of Bergson's theory of time is to be found in divergence from his early opinions. At that time, Bergson was a Spencerian, and he had early wished to complete Spencer. Why Bergson was attracted by Spencer? Because the latter, in the modern scientific way, 'announced a doctrine of evolution, in which the progress of matter toward perceptibility would be traced together with the advance of mind toward rationality, in which the complication of correspondences between the external and the internal would become the very substance of things'.[10]

We must first notice, with Spencer, how closely our ideas of Time and Space are related : "In the phrase 'a great space of time', the magnitude of one serves to denote the magnitude of the other. Conversely, the tourist in Switzerland whose inquiries regarding distance are answered in *stunden*, or hours; and the savage who, in common with the ancient Hebrew, has a place described to him as so many days off, find times used to express space".[11] Uncivilized men express space in terms of Time, civilized men, the reverse. But, though we use co-existences in place of sequences,[12] we should not confuse time with the way we measure it. Because time is irreversibly sequential. Time is a relation between elements of consciousness.[13] It is "the abstract of all relations of position among successive states of consciousness..... the blank form in which these successive states are represented; and which serving alike for each, is not dependent on any".[14]

The abstraction of general time occurs thus : A certain estimated time-distance away from passing states of consciousness, one sensation is present, then another, until the 'place' is separated from particular sensations. When the whole series of places more or less remote from the focus of consciousness has been abstracted, it comes to be 'aggregated into a consciousness of Time, considered as the blank form of all relations of sequence' a real counterpart of space and co-existence.[15]

Regarding the foregoing, Bergson says, 'Duration is always expressed in extensity. The terms that designate time are borrowed from the language of space. When we evoke time, it is space that responds to the appeal.[16]

There is a real space, without duration, in which phenomena appear and disappear simultaneously with our states of consciousness. There is a real duration, the heterogeneous moments of which permeate each other; each moment, however, can be brought into relation with a state of the external world which is contemporaneous with it, and can be separated from the other moments in consequence of this very process. The comparison of these two realities gives rise to a symbolical representation of duration, derived from space. Duration thus assumes the illusory form of a homogeneous medium, and the connecting link between these two terms, space and duration, is simultaneity, which might be defined as the intersection of time and space.[17]

Once we grasp Space and Time as homogeneous forms, we are unable to keep them separated. The pressure of practical life forces us to reduce one to the other. But space and time are both real and delegating space to represent time is symbolical. Here, Bergson agrees with Spencer.[18] Bergson disagrees with Spencer when he coins 'duration' : *i.e.*, a dynamic flow of time is something 'living' and is different from Spencer's static concepts of space and time. Spencer could not give up the Newtonian conception of 'mechanical' time. Bergson disagrees not only with Spencer, but also with the whole powerful modern tradition stemming from Kant. That is to say, Bergson accepts something of Kant, modifies a part, and draws strength together with individuality from opposition to him. In his first book Bergson adopts Kant on space :

'We have assumed the existence of a homogeneous space and, with Kant, distinguished this space from the matter which fills it. With him we have admitted that homogeneous space is a 'form of the sensibility' and we understand by this simply that other minds, *e.g.* those of animals, although they perceive objects, do not distinguish them so clearly either from one another or from themselves. This intuition of a homogenous medium, an intuition peculiar to man, enables us to exter-nalise our concepts in relation to one another, reveals to us the objectivity of things, and thus, in two ways, on the one hand by getting everything ready for language, and on the other by showing us an external world, quite distinct from ourselves, in the perception of which all minds have a common share, foreshadows and prepares the way for social life'.[19]

**Renouvier and Bergson :** It is interesting to note that Renouvier also uses the word duration like Bergson : 'The synthesis of the interval and the limit, or of the instant and time, is *duration*......[20] Duration is thus the synthesis of the interposition of possible instants between two given instants..... Under this relation (of container to content), duration is a quantity, duration is composed of durations, and can be measured by means of a certain duration taken as unity, if one succeeds in fixing the latter in representation in some way. Finally, continuity appears to us as the indefinite divisibility of duration'.[21] As for the measurement of time Renouvier adds, 'it is obtained through movement, on the principle (or synthetic judgement) that equal durations correspond to equal spaces traversed by two identical moving bodies under the same conditions and in the same circumstances'.[22]

For Bergson there *is* time of the nature described by Spencer and Renouvier; but there is another time beneath the mathematical time, a living time :

'We can think of succession without distinction, and think of it as a mutual penetration, an interconnexion and organisation of elements, each one of which represents the whole, and cannot be distinguished from it except by abstract thought. Such is the account of duration which would be given by a being who was ever the same and ever changing, and who had no idea of space'.[23] But, familiar with the latter idea, we introduce it unwittingly into our feeling of pure succession; we set our states of consciousness side by side in such a way as to perceive them simultaneously, no longer in one another, but alongside of one another; in a word, we project time into space, we express duration in terms of extensity, and succession thus takes the form of a continuous line or a chain the parts of which touch without penetrating one another'.[24]

Renouvier took a step in the direction of Bergson's analysis. He held, space is an intuitively given form of phenomena, but 'time is more particularly a form of the facts of empirical consciousness and of memory'.[25]

**Predecessors of Bergson's Concept of 'Duration' :** According to Bergson there are two kinds of time, the one rich, heterogeneous, indivisible, the other poor, homogeneous, divisible, spatial. Had these views of Bergson ever been anticipated? In our answer we have to first refer briefly to Fichte and Hegel, then to :

| | | | |
|---|---|---|---|
| Ravaisson | (1838)[26] | William James | (1886) |
| Balmes | (1846) | James Ward | (1886) |
| Cournot | (1851) | Fouillee | (1883) |
| Delboeuf | (1865) | Guyau | (1885) |
| Lotze | (1878)[27] | | |

**Influence of German Philosophic Systems on Bergson :** The German romantic idealists exerted a lasting influence on French philosophy. It should be recalled that although the German systems culminate in timelessness, enroute they often pass or transcend or synthesise a conception closely related to Bergson's. Fichte, for instance, is drawn into a Heraclitean scepticism : 'There is nothing enduring, either out of me, or in me, but only change'.[28]

Bergson emphasises the difference between himself and the Germans. Spinoza's "Substance", Fichte's "Ich", Schelling's "Absolute", Hegel's "Idea" and Schopenhauer's "Will" are all emptied of meaning as soon as their authors apply them to the whole of things. If we identify duration with the essence of the perceived, which is obviously both repetitious and necessary spontaneity, commingles with mechanism in an impossible fashion.[29] The nature of German systems is to rise through stages. So, in the Hegelian system we have at least five kinds of time : abstract logical process or time, abstract sensuous or natural time, temporal development, which becomes life, which in turn develops from individual into universal history. Referring to the second kind of time Hegel says, "Because things are finite, they are in time; they do not perish because they are in time; rather, things themselves are the temporal—to be so is their objective vocation (Bestimmung). The process of real things itself makes time, therefore; and just as time is called all—powerful, so is it also all—powerless (Wenn die Zeit das Ohnmachtigste)".[30] Time as mathematics is external, paralysed of life.[31] And material nature, Hegel often affirms, is only repetition.[32] Therefore, vital time begins in a dramatic difference. It "preserves itself by and through its separation from ...... inorganic nature, and by the fact that it consumes ...... inorganic nature. Life in the universal fluid medium (inorganic nature), quietly, silently shaping and moulding and distributing the forms in all their manifold detail, becomes by that very activity the movement of those forms, or passes into life *qua* Process".[33] The life of the living individual "is not identical being in a state of repose, but, on the contrary, represents origination, alternation, mediation with another".[34] Hegelianism, therefore when compared with Bergsonism agrees at least in part with it.

**Felix Ravaisson-Mollien :** Next we have to see the influence of Felix Ravaisson-Mollien[35] on Bergson. In fact Bergson himself admits that some of the elements of Ravaisson's doctrine had been retained in his *Creative Evolution.* The attributes of time given by Ravaisson in his *Essai sur l'habitude* are to be examined first. Ravaisson maintains the four following propositions which are fundamental to Bergson's theory of 'real duration' :—1. That to think of a quantity as made up of distinct elements, or to think of a number, is to represent the parts or units as co-existent; 2. That co-existence in turn, can be represented only in the form of spatial juxtaposition; 3. That, consequently, to think of anything as an "extensive", *i.e.*, a divisible, quantity, is to think of it as spatial; and 4. That 'tout ce qui est de l' espace est hors du temps.'

With regard to space Ravaisson's ideas agree with Bergson's; but both of them differ in their concepteion of time. Ravaisson's attitude toward science is instructive. "Science, work of the understanding, traces and constructs the general outlines of the ideality of things. Nature alone, in experience, gives the substantial integrity of experience. Science circumscribes under the extensive or mathematical unity of logical form. Nature, in intensive unity, constitutes the dynamics of reality".[36]

Regarding Bergson like division of science and understanding from matter, intensity, and dynamism Ravaisson tells : 'Since there is nothing in distinct consciousness except under the general condition of movement, and since movement is in time, the general condition, the being of consciousness is being in time. Time is the primary law and necessary form of consciousness. Everything that is in consciousness is therefore a change having its duration in a subject that endures and does not change at all'.[37]

**Balmes :** From Ravaisson we go to Jaime Luciano Balmes, a Spanish ecclesiastic. He published Filosofia Fundamental in 1846. In this book he discusses about time. How can it be distinguished from things, duration from the enduring, succession from what succeeds? According to Balmes wholly abstract time 'has no real existence; to separate it from beings is to destroy it'.[38] To Balmes, one needs actual experience of phenomena before one can 'form the measure' of time; to Bergson, one needs practical experience to excite geometrizing into being. Regardless of the difference between the vocabularies of Balmes and Bergson, the former seems almost to represent a Bergsonian Kant.

**Cournot :** As for the continuity of things we see Antione Augustin Cournot's opinion similar to Bergson's : 'the human spirit is forced, by its organisation and by the form of the instruments it employs, to substitute habitually for the continuity inherent in things an artificial discontinuity, and in consequence to mark degrees, to break up lines, to trace compartments according to artificial and upto a certain point arbitrary rules...... It is the very act of movement that originally gives to the animal a perception of space, suitable to the functions the animal must fill'.[39]

**Delboeuf :** Another thinker who agrees with mobility of being is J. Delboeuf. He also speaks of duration and says that the moments of the duration are neither past, nor present, nor future. And 'every moment is conceived to be distinct from all the moments that precede and follow it in being big with the future......'[40] Delboeuf's 'bigness with the future' calls to our mind the time of *Creative Evolution*, which gnaws into the future and swells as it advances'.

**Hermann Lotze :** Agreeing with Bergson in opposing the 'time-line' Hermann Lotze says, 'Past and future are *not*, and the representation of them both as dimensions of Time is in fact but an artificial projection, which takes place only for our minds eye, of the unreal upon the plane which we think of as containing the world's real state of existence'.[41] According to him time, 'thought of as a line, it would only possess one real point, namely, the present. From it would issue two endless but imaginary arms, each having a peculiar distinction from the other and from simple nullity, *viz.*, Past and Future. The distinction between these would not be adequately expressed by the opposition of directions in shape'.[42] Lotze's usage of 'two endless and imaginary arms' are highly reminiscent of Bergson's refutation in *Time and Free Will* of the usual conceptions of freedom.

**William James and Ward :** Critics of Bergson point out that Bergson's concept of time was derived from his reading of the articles of Ward in *Mind* of 1886 and of William James' in Revue philosophique in 1884.[43] But Bergson denied that he read those articles. We do not doubt Bergson's honesty; but it seems likely that he read a reference to James or Ward on the subject of time. What was true for James was also true for Ward. Ward wrote in *The Realm of Ends* (p. 306), referring to the eleventh edition of his *Psychology* : 'In 1886, three years before publication of Professor Bergson's *Donnees (Time and Free Will),* I had written a long paragraph on this topic, containing *inter alia* the following : "Thus............ there is an element in our concrete time—perception which has no place in our abstract conception of time. In time, conceived as physical, there is no trace of intensity; in time, as psychically experienced, duration is primarily an intensive magnitude." Bergson by his style of language elaborated this theory in his work. Of course Bergson disliked talk of 'intensive magnitude.'

**Fouillée and Guyau :** Of all prominent philosophers Fouillée and his stepson Guyau influenced Bergson most. During the seventy-four years of life-time (1838-1912), Alfred Fouillée wrote about thirty seven books on philosophical problems. He taught that the idea of liberty has the inherent power of growth and self implementation.[44] It is not only an idea, but an *idea-force,* the existence of which is corroborated by the psychologists.[45] Fouillée, in L'Evolutionism des idees-forces (1890), compared ideas to nuclei like the stars and astronomical systems, where the force that lights and moves the world is concentrated and tries to draw everything to itself.[46] By idea he always means a conscious idea. Therefore, consciousness, "is the immediate presence of reality to itself and the internal unrolling of its riches".[47] Mechanism "is precisely the most impoverished and most fragmentary conception of the world. A conception of the world founded on the phenomena of internal life, on the contrary, envelops additional elements : it envelops qualities, a spontaneous activity, a mode of reciprocal connexion other than that which is familiar to us in the sphere of pure mechanism...... It is the material that gives reality a *quantity,* but it is the mental that gives it a quality".[48]

Fouillées' conception of duration is as close as we can get to Bergson's duration. Regarding duration, he says, "......The grasping of duration becomes impossible. How, in effect, explain the feeling of duration if consciousness is a line in which the diverse perceptions exist one outside the other and one after the other, like the lifeless words of a phrase, without our feeling the passage itself from one perception to another and their continuity?..... We here let ourselves be duped by the imagination, which never considers anything but ready made and principally visual images; let us not be duped similarly by pure intelligence, which cannot easily apply itself except to ideas of definite contour, expressed by definite and immutable words. There are instantaneous photographs of the waves of the sea in storm, and these photographs are as immobile as the seas of ice of Mount Blanc : such would be consciousness if it had not the sense of change; ..... when we enjoy, suffer, wish, we have the feeling of the current of life."[49] The similes of the photograph, the 'lifeless words' of a fragmented phrase, and the blending of one into another colour, all of which are to play a major part in the yet unwritten *"Introduction to Metaphysics"*.[50] Fouilée uses the same argument as Bergson against Zeno.[51] He even claims precedence over Bergson in a letter to Augustin Guyau, son of his own philosopher Stepson :

"Before Nietzsche and Mr. Bergson, I had recognised that movement alone is real, that rest is illusory, and that there is nothing really immobile, except for the geometrical figures imagined by us........"[52]

Fouillee remarked that the Bergsonian theory of time is like Guyau's. Guyau's famous little essay, *La Genese de l' idée de temps,* appeared in the *Revue philosophique* of 1885. But Bergson criticised it in the *Revue,* from the standpoint of his own recent *Time and Free will.* However, we have to note Guyau's concept of time which is essentially like Bergson's. Guyau's time is a composite, a 'living and moving depth', or 'course,' a tenseness and transition, pure change, the elemental variety of life, as opposed to the 'passive' and 'reproductive' form that is the 'bed' of time. There are even verbal near—identities. For example, Guyau writes that regular time is in the beginning a fourth dimension of things that occupy space".[53] In *Time and Free Will,* Bergson uses the same words, which recur again in Duree et simultaneite.[54]

So far, we have seen the influence of other philosophers on Bergson with regard to his concept of time and duration. Bergson praised modern physics for escaping the discontinuities of Newtonian physics, and modern mathematics for following motion from within.[55] He compared Einstein's theory of relativity with his theory of duration. *Duree et simultaneite* (1922) expresses Bergson's decision that the paradoxes of relativity are only apparent and that the theses of Einstein begin to prove the natural belief of men in a unique and universal Time, at which Bergson had hinted in *Creative Evolution.*[56] Although there are many different time-tensions, according to Bergson, all human minds perceive in the same way, and therefore live something of the same duration. Implicitly, we imagine human minds throughout the universe. They are close enough to be consecutive. They have the extremity of their fields of experience. Looked at from another vantage point, the many consciousnesses form one rhythm. We eliminate the human minds that served as relays for thought-movement. Only an impersonal and universal time remains,[57] which must have the nature of consciousness.[58]

## 2. BERGSON'S BACKGROUND FOR HIS VIEW OF INTUITION

Bergson affirms that joy is an orientation toward the future. It is an enrichment of sensation, while sorrow faces the past, for it is impoverishment of sensation and idea.[59] Guyau follows this foot-step. For him the eager pressing forward into life, the wealth of sensation and thought accumulated by the living man, is joy itself; and inertia, the worst of crimes, is poverty, sorrow, death.[60]

Bergson defined pleasure and pain in the same way as James : "The attraction of pleasure is nothing but this movement (toward its object) that is begun, and the very keenness of the pleasure, while we enjoy it, is merely the inertia of the organism, which it (the inertia) immerses in it (the pleasure) and rejects every other sensation..... In the moral as in the physical world, attraction serves to define movement rather than to produce it.[61] And we should 'define the intensity of the pain by the very number and extent of the parts of the body which sympathize with it and react, and whose reactions are perceived by consciousness'."[62]

However, Bergson admitted that sensation can be measured and thus agrees with Fechner. In measuring the magnitude of sensation, Fechner had to assumer the equality of all *just noticeable differences* of sensation. Delboeuf countered Fechner's assumption by showing that we can judge directly whether the distance between two sensations is more or less than, or equal to, another distance between two sensations. Thereby he said that he could construct a sensation scale free of arbitrary assumptions. Jules Tannery also held that quality can be measured.[63] Bergson duly acknowledges his debt to Tannery for the above view. But he fought the rationalism of measuring sensations whenever it had metaphysical ambitions. The mathematical psychology and mechanical reasoning according to Bergson cannot account for the drama of human discovery and progress. All the discoveries are the result of 'an immediate intuition, and as such the work of an instant, an appercu, a flash of insight. They are not the result of a process of abstract reasoning, which only serves to make the immediate knowledge of the understanding permanet for thought by bringing it under abstract concepts, *i.e.*, it makes knowledge distinct, it puts us in a position to impart it and explain it to others'.[64]

**Schopenhauer on Intuition :** The above is the voice of Bergson expressed through the words of Schopenhauer, who adds further :

"Only the worst knowledge, abstract, secondary knowledge, the conception, the mere shadow of true knowledge, is unconditionally communicable. Its perceptions were communicable, that would be a communication worth the trouble; but at last every one must remain in his own skin and skull, and no one can help another. To enrich the conception from perception is the unceasing endeavour of poetry and philosophy. However, the aims of man are essentially *pratical;* and for these it is sufficient that what he has apprehended through perception should leave traces in him, by virtue of which he will recognise it in the next case; thus he becomes possessed of worldly wisdom. ........Wisdom proper is something intuitive, not something abstract."[65]

**Cournot :** Cournot when referring to intuition says :

'Plato came before Aristotle : for it lies in the nature of the human spirit that the intuitions of the philosophers precede the organisation of positive science, whose deepest questions the philosopher arrives at in a trice, questions which are in reality the most fundamental, and to which the savant returns later for the co-ordination and explanation of patiently accumulated facts'.[66]

**Bergson's Views**

Intuition according to Bergson in his own words :

'Our intelligence...........can place itself within the mobile reality, and adopt its ceaselessly changing direction; in short, can grasp it by means of that *intellectual sympathy* which we call intuition........ *To philosophise, therefore, is to invert the habitual direction of the work of thought*....... A profoundly considered history of human thought would show that we owe to it all that is greatest in the sciences, as well as all that is permanent in metaphysics...... But metaphysics, which aims at no application, can and usually must abstain from converting intuition into symbols. Liberated from the obligation of working for practically useful results, it will indefinitely enlarge the domain of its investigations'.[67]

Bergson's concern with intuition came to him after he had seen the real time with the eye of the spirit.[68] Intuition is so closely allied with time. Bergson therefore could say : 'I consider the very centre of the doctrine to be : the intuition of duration. The representation of a heterogeneous, qualitative, creative duration is the point from which I have departed and to which I have constantly returned. It demands a very great effort of the mind, the breaking of many frames, something like a new method of thought for the immediate is far from being what is easiest to perceive'.[69]

Bergson's introspection could not be expressed adequately in words. So, he says,-'Intuition is....... a word before which I hesitated a long time. Of all the terms that designate a mode of knowing, it is still the most appropriate; and yet it lends to confusion. Because a Schelling, a Schopenhauer and others have already made appeal to intuition, because they have more or less opposed intuition to intelligence, it might have been thought that I was applying the same method. As if their intuition were not an immediate quest for the eternal! As if, on the contrary, the matter were not first, as I see it, to rediscover true duration. Many are the philosophers who have felt the powerlessness of conceptual thought to attain the depths of spirit. Many, in consequence, those who have spoken of a supra-intellectual faculty of intuition. But, since they have thought that intelligence was operating in time, they have concluded that the surpassing of intelligence consists in emerging from time'.[70]

**Maine de Biran :** Like Bergson, Maine de Biran also talks of life to be stream like and heterogeneous :

'Our existence is sometimes severed by sharply divided epochs, and sometimes its diverse periods succeed one another insensibly and go on, intermingling with a gradation that makes the transition imperceptible. It is certain that our successive existence does not have two like instants. Man, carried by a swift current from his birth until his death, finds no place where to cast anchor'.[71]

Biran says that we can sense the flow of life by internal experience (*experience interieure),* by an intimate sense (*sens intime*) identical with our sense of effort. We get all our knowledge of externalities from this immediate knowledge of the self. Through our actions we perceive nature from the outside. 'In consciousness, on the contrary, it is the same being that acts and sees the act, or rather the act and the view of the act intermingle. The author, the drama, the actor, the spectator, are but one. It is here alone, then, that one can hope to surprise the principle of the act'.[72]

**Felix Ravaisson :** Felix Ravaisson agrees with the above view of Biran. His *report on Philosophy in France in the Nineteenth Century* (1867), in its final pages foreshadowed spiritualism :

'Many signs make it....... permissible to foresee as little distant a philosophic epoch whose general character will be the predominance of what one might call a spiritualist realism or positivism, having for generative principle the spirits' inner consciousness (la conscience que l' sprit prend en lui-meme) of an existence-nothing other than its own action—that it recognises as the source and support of every other existence'.[73]

Bergson called Ravaisson's intuitionism as a 'powerful effort of mental vision to pierce the material envelope of the things and then to read the formula, invisible to the eye, that unrolls and manifests their materiality'.[74]

**Jules Lachelier :** Jules Lachelier, the second great progenitor of French spiritualism also held that the progression of thought as revealed in self-consciousness was the universal principle. Though he was not an intuitionist, he followed the 'dialectical progress of thought' by 'construction' and 'synthesis'.[75]

**Fouillee :** From Ravaisson and Lachelier—and from Schopenhauer, who had also affected Lachelier—the current of intuitionism flowed to Fouillée. But when Bergsonism became powerful, Fouillée fought against the kind of intuitionism that Bergson advocated. To such an extent Fouillée was an intellectualist. However, his doctrine is close to intuitionism : "When we speak of conscious life, we designate by it not *formal* thought alone with its cold and colourless mechanism; no, it is the totality of internal experience, which is the revelation to self of the real existence of things; it is experience as *feeling* and *action*, and as *thought* at the same time, which give us a place among real things and thereby also makes these things exist for us".[76]

**Guyau on Intuition :** Fouillée's doctrine resembles Bergson's in spirit. But his stepson Guyau's description of philosophic intuition is startlingly like Bergson's :

"....... The ideal aim of our method would thus be to replace the artificial divisions and subdivisions by the natural evolutions. For that, the first thing to do is to find and grasp the chief idea (idee maitresse) of the doctrine one wants to expound. This idea or these ideas (for there are sometimes several of them entering more or less into one another) truly give a system its personal character, its unity and life : they are the central point where everything comes to be connected and to which it is necessary to penetrate at the very start......"[77]

Though the views of Bergson and Guyau on intuition are close, they are not identical. For Bergson philosophic progress is by mutations, by sudden leaps and by intuitions. Bergson does not agree with Guyau's conception of continuous evolution of thought. Guyau, for his continuous evolution depends upon intelligence, whereas Bergson for his philosophic progress puts his trust in mysticism. Bergson believed in a 'depth psychology' and so he developed his intuitionism into mysticism.

## 3. BERGSON'S BACKGROUND FOR HIS PSYCHOLOGY

Paracelsus or Theophrastus Hohenheim believed that humans have magnetic connection with the stars. His view that magnets influence us by their emanation was a foreshadowing of Mesmerism. Charles Richet wrote an article in 1875, and in 1884 in the Revue philosophique. In it, he maintained that one person could influence another nearby person through thought alone.[78]

**Bergson on Hypnotism :** When he was very young, Bergson wrote an article 'Unconscious Simulation in Hypnotism' in 1886.[79] Through this article we should not conclude that Bergson was a hypnotist. But his concern with hypnotism had a powerful effect on his philosophy. He wrote as an introduction how he had been drawn to conduct several experiments :

"About two months ago I learned that an inhabitant of Clermont, Mr. V., ........was devoting himself to experiments on hypnotism of young persons from fifteen to seventeen years old, with whom he was obtaining remarkable effects of mental suggestion. Thus, on opening before their eyes a book of which they saw only the cover, he managed to have them divine or read the number of the page he was looking at, even to see words, entire lines. In the cases, rare, moreover, in which the answer was inexact, it was enough to order the subject to read number by number or letter by letter for him to rectify his error. Mr. V........... wanted in vain to make me witness to these experiments, at which I was present in company with Mr. Robinet, assistant at the Faculty of Sciences of Clermont. We ascertained that Mr. V.......... was working with remarkable sureness and in entirely good faith; we resolved nevertheless to repeat the experiments ourselves".[80]

The decisions to which the two experimenters came were that the words were reflected on the cornea of the experimenter and read by the hypnotized subjects. The subjects had great hyperesthesia that they could perceive almost microscopic objects when it was suggested that the objects were large. So, the experimenters concluded that the subject was lying unconsciously in accord with the command of the experimenter. This was possible for the subject because of the experimenter's suggestion to him as a means unconsciously conveyed to him.

**Conscious and Unconscious Activity :** Maine de Biran maintained that unconscious is the feeling of life, with all its affective, representative, and motor 'components' when determined by movements. These movements originate in organic life rather than in the supraorganic self (the true focus of our spiritual personality).[81]

Ravaisson refers to work on hallucination, madness, dreams, phrenology, instinct, and so on in his Report,[82] all a part of psychology. Hartmann's Philosophy of the unconscious, published in 1868, was a powerful new impetus. But Schelling understood how 'in all, even the commonest and most every day production, there co-operates with the conscious an unconscious activity'.[83] Hartmanns's hope was that philosophy 'would seek the golden treasure in the mountain's depths, in the noble ore of its rocky beds, rather than on the surface of the fruitful earth.'[84] This hope of Hartmann influenced the French psychologists. This is evident in Guyau's writings :

"We should recognise that consciousness embraces a quite small portion of life and of action. Even the acts that are completed in full self-consciousness generally have their principle and their first origin in the insensible instincts and in some reflex movements. Consciousness is then only a luminous point in the great obscure sphere of life; it is a small lens grouping several rays of sun into pencils of light and imagining that its focus is the very focus from which the rays diverge. The natural energy of action, before appearing in consciousness, must already have acted beneath it, in the obscure region of instincts".[85]

**'Superficial ego' and 'Deeper self'**

In the same period Bergson's *Time and Free Will* appeared with a similar doctrine of a 'superficial ego' and a 'deeper self'.[86] The superficial ego is culture-created, stable, impersonal.[87] Consciousness is fluid.

'Not all our ideas, however, are thus incorporated in the fluid mass of our conscious states. Many float on the surface, like dead leaves on the water of a pond : the mind, when it thinks them over and over again, finds them ever the same, as if they were external to it. Among these are the ideas which we receive ready made and which remain in us without ever being properly assimilated, or again the ideas which we have omitted to cherish and which have withered away'.[88]

**Philosophy and Psychology**

For Bergson, the deeper stratum of self is something recoverable; it was that to Guyau also. It is necessary to review some of the ideas of Ribot and Binet to know how this intuitionism was furthered by contemporary psychology. Theodule Armand Ribot declared the independence of psychology from philosophy in a review in *English Psychology* (1870). Psychology is "the pure and simple study of those facts that can constitute an independent science." Metaphysicians, by contrast, "are poets, whose aim is the reconstruction of the synthesis of the world".[89]

Ribot rejected Biran's spiritualism : "I am not ignorant that of late years it has been repeated, after Maine de Biran and Jouffray, that, 'the soul knows itself, lays hold on itself, immediately'. But not only have these psychologists passed twenty or thirty years in study before they discover this *immediate knowledge* (which is sufficiently surprising),—the *discovery* does not seem to advance us much; because when we have long and scrupulously sought what this intimate essence thus revealed is, we succeed only in finding such vague expressions as 'absolute activity', 'pure spirit outside of time and space', whence we may conclude that still the clearest part of our knowledge consists in phenomena'."[90]

Even though Ribot rejected Biranian spiritualism with scorn, we should not be tempted to think him at the opposite pole from Bergson because there was a process at the basis of Ribot's work :

"The idea of progress, of evolution, or of development, which of late has become preponderant in all the science, has been suggested by the double study of natural sciences and of history. The scholastic ideas of the immutability of the forms of life, and the uniformity of the epochs of history have given place to a contrary conception. *The doctrine of Heraclitus has been revived and confirmed by the experiences of twenty centuries; all melts, all changes, all moves, all becomes"*.[91]

The universal flow is tempered by habit, memory, heredity and causality. As in the universe, so in the individual, "Nothing that has been can cease to be"[92] (A principle of Bergsonism). How Bergonism is true for memory is dramatically shown by the way in which a drowning man swiftly recalls the whole of his life, even to the smallest details. (Bergson cites Ribot and others, using the same instance as proof).[93] Psychic memory is not independent of the body, but 'the highest and most complex form of organic memory'[94] (Bergson quotes Ribot on this point).[95] From the invariable prolongation of perception into movement, there arises psychic memory and the connection is *'registered'*. So, we have recognition or habit. Consciousness condenses the past[96] and so it is useful. It is a spectator and not an actor. The body perceives and responds by taking an attitude; we consciously attend—that is, we are conscious of the attitude our body has taken : Bergson regards this view of Ribot as correct.[97]

In Bergson's opinion, Ribot's formulation leaves something out.[98] Ribot's explanation of habit-memory or organic memory is not self-sufficient. To be self-sufficient it needs the collaboration of another form of memory. This Bergson calls as "pure memory". This is also unconscious. But it is absolutely retentive and always unique. Consciousness is an organ of choice. It is the *present* accompaniment of *present* action. By drawing on pure memory consciousness helps to direct this action. It also leads that memory up through the different planes of awareness to merge with activity.[99]

According to Ribot, states of consciousness are discontinuous one with another. Each state is limited and therefore associable. (This point is referred to by Bergson in his Matter and Memory many times). Consciousness is also discontinuous in the sense that 'one does not always think'.[100] But psychic phenomena are continuous.

"Every state of consciousness represents only a very feeble portion of our psychic life, because it is at every instant sustained and so to speak pushed by the unconscious states. (Bergson reverses this : it is conscious intelligence that illuminates or 'pulls out' the unconscious states). Every volition, for example, plunges to the deepest depth of our being; the motives that accompany and apparently explain it are never anything but a feeble part of the real cause. (Bergson asserts this plunge for exceptional and moral acts). The same for a great number of our sympathies, and the fact is so clear that the minds most destitute of observation are often astonished at their inability to account for their hatreds and their loves".[101]

Bergson says about this last : 'Just in proposition as we dig below the surface and get down to the real self, do its states of consciousness cease to stand in juxtaposition and begin to permeate and melt into one another, and each to be tinged with the colouring of all the others. Thus, each of us has his own way of loving and hating; and this love or this hatred reflects his whole personality'.[102]

## Influence of French Scientific Psychology on Bergson

The depth psychology of Ribot was incorporated by Bergson with his spiritualism and intuitionism. The intuitionism of Bergson can also be compared to the theories of multiple personalities. For example, the representative of this theory, Binet says :

"We have said that forgetting is often purely relative, true only of a particular mental condition, and not for a different mental condition; we have equally seen that unconsciousness exists only with regard to a certain personality, and ceases for another synthesis of phenomena. In a word, there can be in a single individual a plurality of memories, plurality of consciousness, plurality of personalities; and each of these memories, of these consciousnesses, of these personalities knows only what takes place in its territory. Outside of our consciousness, conscious thought that we ignore may be produced in us; to fix the nature, the importance, the extent of these consciousness seems impossible for the moment; it is possible that consciousness is the privilege of certain of our psychic acts; it is also possible that it is everywhere in our organism; it is even possible that it accompanies all the manifestations of life".[103]

Therefore, the depth psychology evident in *Time and Free Will* and *Matter and Memory* are an almost direct result of Bergson's interest in French scientific psychology, in which Ribot was a path-breaker.

## Body-mind Problem

Now, let us see how Bergson's conclusions on the body-mind relation were anticipated before his *Matter and Memory* appeared. Bergson had an interest in the study of aphasia. A reference to Ravaisson's *Report*[104] is enough to show that the study of psychiatry continued in France. During the 1860s, to go outside the *Report*, many accepted the cases of loss of speech shown by Broca in persons with definitely placed lesions as proof of cerebral localization. Among them was Hughlings Jackson. Jackson's research covers the period from 1864 to 1893. He noted that 'destructive lesions, never cause positive effects, but induce a negative condition which permits positive symptoms to appear'.[105] He observed that words are not really lost. Only the ability to use them for propositional thinking appears to be lost. A woman patient who cried "Fire!" when she saw a fire in the street must have retained far more than the word alone.[106] The faculty of language' cannot be localized 'anywhere except in the whole brain or whole body'.[107]

This idea of Jackson is close to Bergson's idea that, 'that which is commonly held to be a disturbance of the psychic life itself, an inward disorder, a disease of the personality, appears to us, from our point of view, to be an unloosing or breaking of the tie which binds this psychic life to its motor accompaniment, a weakening or an impairing of our attention to outward life'.[108] Jackson also anticipated Bergson's denial of localization of memory images of words.[109]

Vladimir Jankélévitch, a Bergsonian recognised Jackson's anticipation of Bergson. Both Fouillée and Ribot give note to Jackson in their books which Bergson certainly would have read. So, it is worth noticing that of all sciences treated by Bergson, neurobiology comes closest to accepting like views.

## 4. BERGSON'S BACKGROUND FOR HIS CONCEPT OF ÉLAN VITAL

If we trace the origin of Bergson's root in biology, invariably we will also be tracing the origin of Bergson's concept of élan vital. After studying the relation of the brain to memory, thought and action, Bergson immersed himself in biology. This helped him to develop his psychophysiology and to have a vitalistic tradition of his own.

**Development of Vitalism**

Hegel and Schelling spoke often of a life-force struggling upward against the refractoriness of 'matter'. This life-force according to them is embodying itself in increasingly spiritual beings. Lorenz Oken, a biologist was affected by Schelling's romanticism. Ludolf Treviranus, a plant cytologist, thought that behind body and spirit alike there lies an unconscious formative power. Johannes Muller, the famous physiologist, explained the development of living things from an 'organic creative force' different from intelligence. There were many other vitalists among the biologists. Among the philosophers Schopenhauer and Edward von Hartmann were notable vitalists.

At his time in France, Lamarck, an evolutionist, said that all life is motion and the evolution of animals is caused by their inner effort for perfection. By now Paul Joseph Barthez decided that all manifestations of life are to be explained by a general life principle. Later, Bichat thought that life in its essence is unknown. He formulated a kind of vitalism in his well known definition of life as 'the sum of the functions that resist death.' In Sabatier's opinion, 'there is in nature an ideal that can be defined as the development and perfection of spirit in the form of higher and higher individualities...... The living world is no more than an always progressive concentration of psychic energy, diffused everywhere 'as the organizing energy of the universe;'[110] ........the origin of functional adaptations is in 'the continual effort of the will of the animal'.[111]

In 1894, Gustav Wolff conducted an experiment to know whether Darwinism or teleology is true. He extracted the lens from the eye of a water newt. The newt grew another lens from the iris, although the lens had originally developed from skin tissue. Therefore, he concluded that adaptation was 'proved' to be purposeful and Darwinism absurd.[112] After taking note of this experiment and similar ones,

Bergson decided that there must be 'some inner directing principle...... to account for this convergence of effects', which is not possible either on the theory of Darwin or of De Vries.[113] Latent in any part of an organism there is the impulse from which the whole is produced.[114] Coming to the same conclusion like Bergson, Driesch built upon it a difficult theory of vitalism in which there is the *entelechy*, an individualizing supervisory force, which 'carries its purpose within itself' and makes of the organism more than an aggregate. His theory was widely welcomed in Germany.

If we turn to the biological and cosmological speculations of the philosophers, we shall note that parallels to several of the leading ideas expressed in *Creative Evolution*, they show a general structural likeness to the Bergsonism of Biology. Even Spencer, termed by vitalists as their archenemy, became a kind of agnostic vitalist. He said, 'we are obliged to confess that life in its essence cannot be conceived in physico-chemical terms..... We find it impossible to think of Life as imported into the unit of protoplasm from without; and yet we find it impossible to conceive it as emerging from the co-operation of the components..... But..... our surface knowledge continues to be a knowledge valid of its kind'.[115]

Spencer's agnosticism had been self-defeating. Bergson's élan vital finds its precedence in the love of Empedocles, the fire-tension of the Stoics, the conatus of Spinoza, or the will to live of Schopendhauer. Let us first listen to the biologists. According to Claude Bernard,...... "In every living germ there is a creative idea that develops and manifests itself through organisation. Throughout all its duration the living being rests under the influence of this same vital creative force, and when it can no longer realize itself death arrives. Here as everywhere, all derives from the Idea, which, alone, creates and directs".[116] However, Bergson does not agree with the teleological tinge of Bernard's summation.

**Élan Vital : Lalande and Bergson :** The very expression

*élan vital,* made world-famous by Bergson, was used in a similar connection by Lalande which Bergson had read.[117] Lalande wrote : 'The living being is characterized by a course of development absolutely without example in the inorganic : embryonic germ, differentiation of tissues, adult state, senility and death. It struggles for life, it deforms itself more or less in this struggle. And according to every appearance, the species behave in this life the individuals, having a modest start, an *élan vital* that tends to multiply them without limit, finally a triumph more or less complete followed by regression and decadence'.[118]

Following this élan back into its cosmic beginnings we find, metaphorically speaking, 'an immense reservoir of life' that jets out unceasingly, and whose jets condense into worlds and fall back, while the persistent impulse pushing against them gives rise to the evolution of living species. From a closer range, life is a fragmenting shell whose particles themselves explode without end, push fiercely against the resistance of their containing matter.[119] More specifically, the animal is enabled to move by its ability to release energy suddenly, energy derived from solar radiation and stored in plants.[120]

This expression of Bergson can be traced back to Neo Platonism, in which matter is diffusion of reality.[121] Not going so far back into history, we shall begin with the poetic expression of Schopenhauer[122] and Hartmann.

### Schopenhauer's 'will to live'

'Every glance at the world, to explain which is the task of the philosopher, confirms and proves that *will to live.........* is the only true expression of its inmost nature. Everything presses and strives toward *existence,* if possible *organised existence, i.e., life,* and after that to the highest possible grade of it. In animal nature it then becomes apparent that *will to live* is the keynote of its being, its one unchangeable and unconditional quality. Let any one consider this universal desire for life, let him see the infinite willingness, facility, and exuberance with which the will to live presses impetuously into existence under a million forms everywhere and at every moment, by means of fructification and of germs, nay, when these are wanting, by means of *generatio acquivoca*, seizing every opportunity, eagerly grasping for itself every material capable of life....... In vain do we seek by contemplating her (nature) for an end of this restless striving, this ceaseless pressing into existence, this anxious care for the maintenance of the species'.[123]

**Hartmann**

Hartmann gives in the following why the creative force materialises itself :

'It might appear to the superficial observer as if the resistance which the unconscious finds in inorganic matter to its organising activity were an instance against the all-unity of the unconscious. This is, however, by no means the case. We have seen above that the strife and struggle of the individualised natural forces or formations of the unconscious is a necessary condition for the coming to pass of the objective phenomenal world and for the origin of consciousness in particular; here occurs only a special case of this general truth...... The unconscious must, therefore, previously create a matter in order to be able to create organisms, and, moreover, a matter subjected to exceptionless laws, because only in such is the setting up of accessory mechanisms possible, which always perform the same task. That, however, such a matter, comforting itself according to its own laws, which of itself does not tend to the formation of organisms, opposes a certain resistance to the activity of the unconscious, is self-evident, and it is no wonder that this resistance can under certain circumstances assume such proportions that the unconscious, interested only in the universal, not in the single case, forbears to master the difficulties that present themselves, since it more easily attains it by a different path, or attains indeed at other places, often enough for the purposes of the whole process, the same end.'[124]

In the above words of Hartmann it is not difficult to see in the process Bergson's *élan,* working in various directions through self-created and resistant matter toward freedom, although some of its forms may crystallise or even retrogress.[125] Hartmann even has an analogue to Bergson's theory that each of the lines of evolution must continue to diverge more and more from the other[126]—the laws of 'dichotomy' and 'twofold frenzy' in the new wording of the theory in *Two Sources of Morality and Religion.* He says, 'The unconscious must (apart from its continuous interposition in every organic formation, thus also in all generation) display a direct activity in the progressive development of the organisation : on the one hand, in order with the new germs to *call forth* the variations that do *not accidentally* arise; and, on the other hand, to preserve from being *again obliterated* by crossing the variations that have arisen, which belong to its plan, but do not aid the *competition* of the organism in the struggle for existence'.[127] The increasing variety of life is not a mere matter of utility. It is also divergence to fulfil the urge of the *élan* to diversify itself incessantly as it tries to gain embodied freedom.

### Renouvier and Ravaisson

Hartmann wrote the *Philosophy of the unconscious* in 1868. But even four years earlier Renouvier finished the first edition of his *Essais de critique générale.* In this book he gives an account of the 'radical' and *jetlike spontaneity of life.* Turning then to Ravaisson we have him saying that, 'the whole series of beings is nothing other than the continous progression of the successive powers of one and the same principle, which envelops them one and all in the hierarchy of the forms of life...........'[128]

**Cournot**

Antoine Augustin Cournot with a similar tone, like Bergson, speaks of life and evolution : There is in life, he argues, an organic and creative force that is the first cause of organic beings; it exists in the germ before any organs are formed and persists in the adult without being 'chained' to any organ. The instinct of animals is also a revelation of this force that works without consciousness, but according to rational laws.[129] Such instinct coordinates living beings in space and time : the organisation of the foetus is appropriate both to its present and to its future activities; the bird instinctively gathers nest materials before it lays eggs.[130] Put in another way, the living body is a union in which each part is contained in the whole, whereas inert particles are exterior to one another. The 'plastic force and vital energy' cause the rudimentary organs of the embryo to meet and associate, tissues to reproduce, organs to regenerate.[131]

Regarding Bergson's theory that evolution takes place in divergent paths and not in a single direction, Cournot says, 'The great *branches* of the animal kingdom present such diversities of plan that *it would be absurd to wish to range them in the same series.* There are molluses more perfect than others in their organisation, and insects of an organisation higher than that of other insects : but how judge the relative perfection of the type of the insect?'[132] The same is true of plants;[133] and it is ridiculous to think them created for animals.[134]

Bergson when emphasising the divergent directions of élan vital in course of its evolution says that 'the cardinal error, which from Aristotle onwards, has vitiated most of the philosophies of rational life, three successive degrees of the development of one and the same tendency, whereas they are three divergent directions of an activity that has split up as it grew'.[135] This point as we have discussed had already been seen by Cournot.

**F. Marin**

One further source for the biological and cosmological concept *i.e.*, élan vital of Bergson is the article written by F. Marin[136] in which he begins with a question : 'What is a species, and above all a fixed species, in this moving continuity (of life)? The term instantly loses its significance and becomes purely ideal : it is a type fixed by the mind at an arbitrarily chosen moment; it is an immobilised frame (cadre), marked out in the perpetual change of the individual....... In the mobile continuity of the real we see for the first time this scientific activity of the intelligence at work, which consists of grasping the continuous in the form of successive discontinuous phases alone'.[137]

Marin, in 1901 applied Bergsonism to biology before Bergson himself had done so. Marin stated that there is in the universe an effective resistance, a purely negative and brutal environment.[138] ........ Although environments differ widely, identical organs are produced in them, which demonstrates the superiority of the internal impulse over the material environment.[139]

So, Bergson's concept of vital impulse or élan vital was previously, in one form or other discussed by his predecessors. This, however, does not mean that we are doubting Bergson's originality because Bergson's application of élan vital to the theory of evolution is quite different from his predecessors. Bergson's conception of the vital force is something unique in his philosophy.

## 5. BERGSON'S BACKGROUND FOR HIS VIEWS ON MORALITY AND RELIGION

In each of Bergson's successive books, the facts are drawn from a new science, physiological psychology in *Matter and Memory*, biology in *Creative Evolution*, and sociology or ethnology in *The two Sources of Morality and Religion*. In his last work, he discusses Lévy—Bruhl, Westermarck, Van

Gennep, and a few others. He preserves freedom from dogmatic reaffirmation of their theses.

Among the French sociologists who influenced Bergson most to write *The two Sources,* Emile Durkheim ranks first. Durkheim was the father of French sociology and ethnology. It was he, who founded the *Anee sociologique* in 1898, and furnished a basis for innumerable later speculations with his *Elementary Forms of the Religious Life* (1912). He holds it axiomatic that 'society is a reality *sui generis;* it has its own peculiar characteristics ......... The representations which express it have a wholly different content from the purely individual ones.' Such an axiom is exaggeration according to Bergson because institutions, language, and customs are not only social deposits but also the prolongations of individual minds which prefigured in them; the individual is made for social life.[140]

There are also points of agreement between Bergson and Durkheim. Bergson's analysis of moral obligation and closed morality is at the least conceived like obligation and society in their Durkheimian outlines. According to Durkheim, public opinion is as much inside as outside us; we are human because each one of us contains humanity. Most fundamental in our internal humanity are the religious beliefs, something belonging to the group and constructive of it. "A religion is unified system of beliefs and practices relative to sacred things, that is to say, things set apart and forbidden-beliefs and practices which unite into one single moral community called a church, all those who adhere to them."[141] Bergson says, 'Each of us belongs as much to society as to himself......... We are in continuous contact with other men whom we resemble, and united to them by a discipline which creates between them and us a relation of interdependence........ Social solidarity exists only in so far as a social ego is superadded, in each of us, to the individual self. To cultivate this social ego is the essence of our obligation to society'.[142] Kant's "categorical imperative" really implies social solidarity as reflected in habits of obedience, so that it may truthfully be said that half of our moral obligation is social pressure. (The other half, not called "obligation", has the impulsive, leaping flames of emotion within it, or at least the warm ashes left by the flames.) Religion is largely social. The discipline of repeated exercises, the rites and ceremonies, react on and strengthen the beliefs that inspire them. This disciplinary, ritual religion, static religion, "is a defensive reaction of nature against what might be depressing for the individual, and dissolvent for society, in the exercise of intelligence," against death, that is, against little—availing initiative, and egotism. The greater part of our strength, steadiness of effort, and unbroken tension of energy flow from society.[143]

If we want to see how close Bergson's definition of 'static religion' is to Durkheim's, we must push the comparison further. According to Durkheim, social ways of action reflect in each individual mind the added vigour derived from many minds. A man of belief gains strength to endure and conquer trials of existence; his faith, the strength of his strength, comes from the cult. "There can be no society which does not feel the need of upholding and reaffirming at regular intervals the collective sentiments and the collective ideas which make its unity and its personality. Now, this moral remaking cannot be achieved except by means of reunions, assemblies and meetings where the individuals, being closely united to one another, reaffirm in common their common sentiment'.[144]

Therefore, we may conclude that Bergson's conception of moral obligation and 'static religion' was drawn from Durkheim or his school, which was the dominating school in France. We should not also forget, however, that Durkheim well knew, 'those hours of creative effervescence, in the course of which new ideas arise and new formulae are found which serve for a whole as a guide to humanity'.[145] While Bergson preferred to believe that religious progress rests in mysticism and escapes science, Durkheim believed, on the contrary, that religious progress is a synthesis created by society and embedded in its individuals.[146]

## Morality of Freedom

Bergson's sociology is differentiated from the Durkheimian by his psychology and mysticism. Bergson's interest in psychology led him to consider mysticism with more attention. Apart from the influence of Durkheim on Bergson, there were also others whose influence on Bergson is not so small. French spiritualism disposed Bergson to a morality of freedom and union with others. Fouillée accentuated his natural belief in a dynamic will, and Guyau pushed on to all—embracing fecundity, interpenetration of souls, and immorality. Both to Guyau and Bergson these views came easily because of the revelation of the subconscious by psychology, with all the associated theories of hypnotism, suggestion, and hysteria.

## Lachelier

We shall see how the freedom of idea took root in Bergson's *Two Sources*. Lachelier spoke of the individual liberty thus : "We are free only because we are a *self*, or (because) there is in us something anterior to perception and to the laws that govern it...... The will..... is free because it is of its own essence to will itself and to be cause of itself....... The will is the principle and the hidden centre (fond) of all that exists".[147]

## Fouillée

This was also the point about which Fouillée says, "The problem of individual liberty is none other than that of *individuation* : one cannot hope to resolve it theoretically and metaphysically with certitude; it takes scientific form only in the following formula : Until what point and by what series of middle-terms can we individualise ourselves?"[148]

**Bergson on Freedom of Idea**

The character of freedom according to Bergson : "We are free when our acts spring from our whole personality, when they have that indefinable resemblance to it which one sometimes finds between the artist and his work".[149] So, Fouillée and Bergson agree that freedom is maximum self-expression. But merely a likeness in idea does not prove an influence.

**Bergson on Fouillées Works on Morality and Idea-force**

In 1905, Bergson wrote to Fouillée of a book on morality the latter had published a short while before : "I have read your work from one end to the other with an always growing interest. It is, in a seductive form and in a language of which you have the secret, a very strong and penetrating critique of the moralities called scientific."[150]

Bergson was still more enthusiastic on the publication of La Morale des idées-forces in 1907 : "How rich in ideas, suggestive, and strong your new work appears to me!...... It is indispensable, as you so well show, to take account of all the given, of *integral* experience, internal as well as external, and not alone of that which is, but of that which *tends* to be. Your conception of the *idea-force* without doubt comprehends the solution of many difficulties. And your analysis of consciousness, in establishing the solidarity of the consciousness of everyone with that of others, demonstrates how the whole essential of morality is *performed* in *nature*."[151]

The phrase, "solidarity of the consciousness of everyone with that of others" is peculiarly significant, for it is the kernel of Bergson's morality.

**Universal Consciousness : Guyau and Bergson**

Regarding Bergson's interest in consciousness we have Guyau according to whom there are the two irreducible factors of life : 1. Fecundity and 2. Sympathy.

"Life is a fecundity, and reciprocally, fecundity is life to the full, is true existence. There is a certain generosity inseparable from life, and without which one dies, one dries up inside. One must flourish; morality, disinterest, is the flower of human life.

Charity has always been represented as a mother who gives her breast swollen with milk to her babies;[152] charity is really identical with overflowing fecundity; it is like a maternity too expansive to stop with the family. The breast of the mother has need of a void mouths that drain it; the heart of the truly human being also has need of making itself gentle and helpful to all."[153]

With regard to the interpenetration of consciousness Guyau says, "..........there would be mutual penetration so intense that......... one would come to live at the very heart of another....... In fact, one can imagine much more subtle and direct means of communication and sympathy than exist today between different individuals. The science of the nervous and cerebral systems has only just begun; as yet we only know the unhealthy exaltations of this system, the sympathies and suggestions of hypnotism; but we already foresee a whole world of phenomena in which....... a communication of consciences tends to produce itself, and even, when the mutual wills consent to it, a sort of absorption of personalities one within the other".[154]

Bergson, by the time of *Creative Evolution,* was suggesting that the "interpenetrating potentialities" of the "rising wave" of consciousness might enable us to overcome even death.[155] He spoke with conscious vagueness. But this was with unmistakable similarity to Guyau.

### Bergson's Root in his Conception of Mysticism

The new and the most significant fact of Bergson's *The two Sources of Morality and Religion* is his discovery of the Christian mystics. In 1905 he wrote to Fouillée that he was dissatisfied with both the 'scientific' and the Kantian ethics. "The difficulty for me is to find something intermediate between this (scientific) morality whose insufficiency you have so well demonstrated and the *a priori* morality of pure obligation. I well sense that the truth should be between the two, but I disentangle them only confusedly, and the moral problem is one of those for which I have not as yet arrived at an even approximate solution that satisfies me".[156]

In Bergson's conception of mysticism there is the dynamic quality of true absorption in God. For this idea Bergson himself acknowledged his deepest conscious obligation to three philosophers : 1. Plotinus, 2. Maine de Biran and 3. Ravaisson. We have not yet seen Plotinian influence on Bergson.

The relevant Plotinian beliefs may be put in a series of brief quotations : (a) "Sense-Perception, Discursive-Reasoning and all our ordinary mentation are foreign to the soul....... If we mean to discern the nature of the Soul we must strip it free of all that has gathered about it.

Bergson could have compared the encrusted self to the sea-god Glaucus, just as Plotinus did in this connection. Only the beauty of sight and sound that enable us to discover the God beneath his seaweed-mantle. But imagery is insufficient to do more than attend and foreshadow truth : (b) "In sum we may safely gather that while the Intellective-Act may be attended by the Imaging Principle, it is not to be confounded with it."

Like Bergson, Plotinus thought the true self would reveal itself through spontaneous moral action rather than through deeds springing from ratiocination : (c) "In a feat of courage there can be no sense either of the brave action or of the fact that all that is done conforms to the rules of courage.... So, that it would even seem that it is exercised, and that in the degree in which these unobserved they are purer and have more effect, more vitality."

According to Bergson we are free when our acts spring from our whole selves. Such acts are unencumbered with materiality or spatiality, as Bergson would more often say : (d) "What enters into Matter ceases to belong to itself, comes to belong to Matter."

For Plotinus, Matter, the Measureless, is evil. But Bergson calls it the Measured. Both Bergson and Plotinus agree on the point that 'matter' is the concept—limit of spiritlessness: (e) Matter........ It is merely a phantom or shadow of space...... It is a ghostly thing incapable alike of staying or going since it has drawn no force from the Divine : and, so, all its pretense of existence is a lie."[157]

Although the First Existent of the Trinity is so strict a unity that it cannot be said to have any quality, the Intellectual-Principle, second member of the Trinity, is inexhaustibly creative : (f) "It overflows, and this overflowing is creative. Imagine a spring which has no commencement, giving itself to all the rivers, never exhausted by what they take, ever tranquilly its full self."

The third member of the Trinity, the All-Soul, makes up the universally present and compresent forms of life, in a somewhat Bergsonian way (and in just the same way as Lachelier) : (g) "The universe is very varied....... It is a being awake and alive at every point........ Each thing has its own peculiar life in the All, though we, because our senses do not discern the activity going on inside wood and stone, deny the life."

It is life and sympathy that draw us all together : (h) "We share each other's feelings; if we see another in distress we suffer with him; we are irresistibly impelled to form friendships."

This union is a kind of inner-soul radiance, like fire admitting no contamination or cooling, and penetrative of all else : (i) "And one that shall know this vision—with what passion of love shall he not be seized, with what pang of desire, what longing to be molten into one with this, what wondering delight!"

It is Plotinus who lit the flame by which Ravaisson and Bergson were enkindled, and probably Guyau too. Bergson admitted that Plotinus looked "upon the promised land." But Plotinus "did not reach the point where, as contemplation is engulfed in action, the human will becomes one with the divine will."[158] Plotinus was not an active mystic.

Bergson calls attention to his indebtedness for active mysticism to two writers, Henri Delacroix and Evelyn Underhill.[159] Besides the above philosophers, William James' *The Varieties of Religious Experience* also played an important role in Bergson's *The two Sources of Morality and Religion.*

## REFERENCES


1. William James : *The Letters of William James*, II, 290-91.
2. F. Nicolardot : *A propos de Bergson*, p. 160; *Flore de Gnose*, pp. 112-18.
3. G. Dumesnil : *'La Sophistique contemporaine'*, Amitee de France, 1912.
4. J. Benda : *Revue de Paris*, CXII (May 15, 1915), 187. C. Dryssen, *Bergson und die deutsche Romantik.*
5. A. Kann : *Henri Bergson und meine Ideen.*
6. 'The theory of intuition, which you stress far more than that of duration, did not come to my mind until rather long after the latter, from which it derives, and through which alone it can be understood.' (From a letter to Harold Höffding, in Höffding's La Philosophie de Bergson, p. 161).
7. Report of a visit of M. Gremil to Bergson, M.F., CVIII (1914), 397.
8. J. Tannery, Science et philosophie, 3rd ed. First published in Revue scientifique, March 13, April 24, 1874.
9. '...... I have not had the pleasure of being his pupil, but I should nevertheless consider him as my teacher. I have been devoted to him since my earliest youth, and throughout my whole career I have cherished a fervent admiration for him together with a profound gratitude. I was still, in fact, on the college benches when I read his thesis on *The Basis of Induction* (Le Fondement de l'induction).... From a letter of Bergson, Bulletin, XXXI (1931), p. 123.
10. *Creative Evolution*, p. 363.
11. Herbert Spencer : *The Principles of Psychology* (2nd ed.).
12. *Ibid.*, p. 208.
13. *Ibid.*, pp. 208-9.
14. Herbert Spencer : *The Principles of Psychology* (2nd ed.), pp. 21, 337.
15. H. Spencer : *The Principles of Psychology*, pp. 210-11.

16. La Pensée et le mouvant, p. 9. The introduction to this group of essays is Bergson's account of his philosophical development.
17. Bergson : *Time and Free Will*, p. 110.
18. A minor similarity between Spencer and Bergson is their admission of different times for different individuals. Spencer notes that the rhythms of our vital functions and of our locomotion determine the sense of time we have. Therefore, time is different for different species, and to a certain extent is varied by individual experience (*Principles of Psychology*, Vol. II, Part I, pp. 213-14). In Bergson's terms : 'It is possible to imagine many different rhythms, which, slower or faster, measure the degree of tension or relaxation of different kinds of consciousness, and thereby fix their respective places in the scale of being' (*Matter and Memory*, p. 275). This distinction becomes the basis of *Creative Evolution.*

    If Bergson's concept is wider, deeper, there is still no reason to belittle the similarity. The one (Spencer's) is more influenced by scientific psychology, the other by introgerm of the second.
19. Bergson : *Time and Free Will*, p. 236.
20. Renouvier employs the same word as Bergson, duree.
21. C. Renouvier, Essais de critique générale. Premier essai (1854), pp. 125, 137-38.
22. *Ibid.*, p. 208. Afterward, in La Nouvelle Monadologie, Renouvier defined the laws of time as 'the general relation of the *before* and *after* to the present that has the instant as limit.... Instants are merely the limits or ends of a *duration*, or stretch of time' (pp. 8-9, quoted in Gunn, *Time*, p. 152). Bergson cites Renouvier, though in a different connection, in *Time and Free Will* (p. 237) Renouvier begins to sound very much like Bergson in *Le Personnalisme* (1903). Time, he there says, is flowing and variable, linked with the essential characteristics of individuality. All the same, we identify time with uniform movement with space. 'Thanks to scientific abstraction, duration has had number applied to it by the interposition of extensity' (p. 371).
23. Lionel Dauriac, a Renouverian, had made the same assumption of a 'pure spirit freed of all relation with space, subject to the sole form of time' seven years before Bergson. Such a being could have no conception of number and extensive quantity, because our states of mind are heterogeneous and interpenetrative (La Critique philosophique, Tannery, Dauriac depreciated psychophysics.
24. Bergson : *Time and Free Will*, p. 101.
25. Renouvier, *op.cit.*, p. 140.
26. The date refers to the work under discussion.
27. Lotze's Metaphysik of 1841 was quite a different work. The English translation of *Matter and Memory* (p. 50) gives the reference to the book of 1878, which contains the passage in question.

28. J.G. Fichte : *The Vocation of Man*, Part II, p. 89.
29. La Pensée et le mouvant, pp. 59-60. Only here does Bergson devote more than a casual mention to the Germans with whom he is often affiliated.
30. G.W. Hegel : *System der Philosophie (Encyclopaedie)* Part II, para. 258.
31. *Ibid.*, paras 254-58.
32. Bergson writes of 'pure homogeneity, that pure *repetition* by which we define materiality' (*Introduction to Metaphysics*, p. 63).
33. Hegel : *Phenomenology* (trans. Baillie), pp. 221-23.
34. Hegel : *Philosophy of Religion* (trans. Speirs and Sanderson), III, 323.
35. For the influence of Ravaisson on Bergson see A.O. Lovejoy's "Some Antecedents of the Philosophy of Bergson" *Mind*, Vol. XXII (1913), pp. 465-483.
36. J. Ravaisson : "De l' habitude, M.M." (1894), p. 34.
37. *Ibid.*, p. 16.
38. The account of Balmes' theory is summarised from Lechalas, pp. 164-69.
39. A. Cournot, Essai, Vol. I (1851), para, 188.
40. H. Ulrici, Compendium der Logik, p. 77; quoted in J. Delboeuf, Essai de logique scientifique, pp. 151-53.
41. H. Lotze, *Metaphysic* (ed. Bosanquet), I, p. 335.
42. *Ibid.*, p. 31.
43. The French summary of William James' articles is "Sur quelques omissions dans la psychologie d' observation interieure."
44. A. Fouillée, La Liberté et le determinisme (3rd ed.), pp. 230f.
45. *Ibid.*, p. 233.
46. A. Fouillée, L' Evolutionisme des idees-forces, p. XCII.
47. *Ibid.*, p. 291.
48. *Ibid.*, p. 291.
49. A. Fouillée, La Psychologie des idees—forces, II, 84-85.
50. Bergson : *Introduction to Metaphysics*, pp. 5, 28, 13.
51. Fouillée, *op.cit.*, II, 86.
52. A. Guyau, La Philosophie et la sociologie d' Alfred Fouillée, p. 212.
53. Guyau, La Genése, pp. 73-74.
54. Bergson : Essai sur les donnees immediates de la, conscience (*Time and Free Will)*, p. 83. Bergson : Duree et simultaneite, p. 78.
55. Bergson : *Matter and Memory*, pp. 265-66; An *Introduction to Metaphysics*, pp. 70-72.
56. Bergson : Duree et simultaneite (2nd ed.), p. viii.
57. *Ibid.*, pp. 58-59.
58. *Ibid.*, p. 62.
59. *Time and Free Will*, pp. 10-11. 'Wherever there is joy', says Bergson, 'there is creation; the richer the creation, the deeper the joy' ('Life and Consciousness,' *Mind-Energy*, p. 29).

60. J.M. Guyau, Esquisse d'une morale sans obligation ni sanction, pp. 12-30.
61. *Time and Free Will*, p. 38.
62. *Ibid.*, p. 36.
63. J. Tannéry : Science et philosophie (3rd ed.), pp. 130, 140 Originally published in the *Revue scientifique*, March 13, April 24, 1875.
64. Schopenhauer, *The World as Will and Idea*, I, 27.
65. Schopenhauer : *The World as Will and Idea*, III, pp. 248, 249. *Cf.* Hartmann, Philosophy of the Unconscious, where he speaks of the 'clair voyant intuition' (I, 114) and the discovery and creation of the beautiful, which originate in unconscious process (*ibid.*, p. 291).
66. A.A. Cournout : Traité, Vol. I (1861), para. 226.
67. Bergson : *Introduction to Metaphysics*, pp. 69, 70, 71.
68. 'I penetrated..... into the domain of internal life, in which I had been uninterested until then'—*i.e.*, until after the finding of duration (La Pensee et le mouvant, p. 10).
69. Letter to Hoffding, in his La Philosophie de Bergson, p. 160. Bergson's intuition can be compared with Schelling's praise of artistic intuition. Philosophic intuition is higher than the artistic intuition to Bergson, because, he says, artistic intuition begins in images and does not penetrate as deeply. Hegel places philosophy above art for the same reason—that philosophy dispenses with sensuous images.
70. La Pensée at le mouvant, p. 33. This quotation is important because it shows that Bergson was occupied with the German idealists at the time of definition of his thought.
71. Maine de Biran : Oeuvres (Tisserand), I, p. 74.
72. J. Ravaisson : "De l' habitude", M.M., XII (1894), 10.
73. J. Ravaisson : Rapport sur la philosophie en France au XIX siecle (ed. of 1885), p. 275.
74. Bergson, 'Notice sur la vie et les Oeuvres de M. Felix Ravaisson—Molien', p. 677.
75. J. Lachelier, Oeuvres, I, 218.
76. A. Fouillée, L' Evolutionisme des idées—forces, p. 279.
77. See J.M. Guyau, La Morale d'Epicure (6th ed., 1917), pp. 4-5. Bergson in his, 'Notice sur la view et les Oeuvres de M. Felix Ravaisson' uses the words idée maitresse (*e.g.* p. 678). The intuition is indescribable and the 'chief idea' is the closest verbal approximation to intuition.
78. Binet and Féré : *Animal Magnetism*, p. 64.
79. This was Bergson's fourth article. The three previous ones were 'Le Rire : de quoi rit-on? Pourquoi rit-on?' (1884); the 'Introduction' to Extraits de Lucréce (1884); 'La Politessee' (1885).
80. Bergson : "De la simulation inconsciente dans l'hypnotisme", R. Ph., XXII (1886), p. 525.
81. Maine de Biran : Oeuvres, Vol. I (1920), Preface by P. Tisserand, pp. ii-iii.

82. Rapport sur la philosophie en France, pp. 178 ff., 202 ff. Ravaisson thought psychology in the domain of philosophy.
83. Schelling, Werke, I, Part III, 624; quoted in E. von Hartmann, Philosophy of the Unconscious, I, 25; see also p. 24.
84. E. von Hartmann, *op. cit.*, I, 2.
85. Esquisse d'une morale sans obligation ni sanction, p. 10. In the same book (pp. 44-45), Guyau refers to posthypnotic suggestion as revealed by Charcot and Richet.
86. Bergson : *Time and Free Will*, p. 125.
87. *Ibid.*, p. 132.
88. Bergson : *Time and Free Will*, p. 135.
89. T. Ribot : *English Psychology*, pp. 15, 14.
90. *Ibid.*, pp. 16-17.
91. English Psychology, p. 25. Italics not in the original.
English Psychology preceded *Time and Free Will* by 26 years.
92. Ribot, L'Hérédité psychologique, conclusion.
93. Bergson : *Matter and Memory*, p. 200.
94. Ribot : *Diseases of the Memory*, p. 202.
95. Bergson : *Matter and Memory*, p. 111.
96. Ribot : Les Maladies de la personnalité, pp. 18-19.
97. Bergson : *Matter and Memory*, pp. 122 ff.
98. *Ibid.*, p. 122.
99. *Ibid.*, p. 319.
100. Ribot, Les Maladies de la personnalité, p. 8.
101. *Ibid.*, p. 13.
102. Bergson : *Time and Free Will*, p. 164.
103. A Binet, Les Altérations de la personnalité, pp. 322-23.
104. See pp. 178-79. He there records the establishment in 1843 of the Annales medico-psychologiques, journal de l'anatomie, de la physiologie et de la pathologie due système nerveuse, destine a recueilller tous les documens relatifs a l' alienation mentale, ause nevroses et a la medicine legale des aliénés.
105. Quoted in T. Weisenburg and K.E. McBride, Aphasia, p. 12. Bergson thought that lesions destroy the ability to guide oneself in life and permit latent, positive, previously censored conditions to appear.
106. Quoted in T. Weisenburg and K.E. McBride, Aphasia, p. 13. 'When the cerebral lesion is severe, and the word-memory is deeply affected, it may happen that a more or less vigorous stimulus, an emotion, for example, will suddenly bring back the recollection which had seemed lost for ever' (Bergson, 'The Soul and the Body', *Mind-Energy*, p. 65.
107. Weisenburg and McBride, *op. cit.*, p. 16.
108. Bergson : *Matter and Memory*, pp. XIV-XV (Introd. of 1910).
109. *Ibid.*, pp. 131 ff.
110. L'Année biologique, VIII (1903), 441-42 (A. Sabatier).

111. *Ibid.*, VIII (1903), 448 (C. Mary)
112. H. Driesch, *The History and Theory of Vitalism*, pp. 174-76.
113. Bergson; *Creative Evolution*, pp. 75-76.
114. *Ibid.*, pp. 13-14.
115. H. Spencer, The Principles of Biology (rev. ed., 1898). pp. 120, 122-23.
116. C. Bernard, Introduction à l' étude de la médecine experimentale (1865), pp. 151 ff.; quoted in Renouvier, Essais de critique generale. Troisiéme essai (ed. 1892), p. 219.
117. A. Lalande, La Dissolution opposée à l' évolution (1899) is called 'rich in facts and in ideas' in a footnote to *Creative Evolution*, pp. 246-47. Bergson goes on to reject Lalande's thesis that opposed to evolution.
118. A Lalande, La Dissolution (ed. 1899), p. 399.
119. Bergson : *Creative Evolution*, pp. 247, 98.
120. *Ibid.*, pp. 115 ff., 253 ff.
121. R. Berthelot, Un Romantisme utilitaire, pp. 98-99, 122.
122. Bergson thought that the 'will to live' of Schopenhauer was an 'empty concept' when true duration was neglected (*Two Sources*, p. 105), and that Schopenhauer's Nevertheless, this does not diminish the likeness of Schopenhauer's 'will' to Bergson's élan. Even on the subject of time Schopenhauer vacillated (*cf.* Gunn, The Problem of Time, pp. 121-27). Bergson had read Schopenhauner, at least on, by 1901 (*Mind-Energy*, p. 91).
123. A. Schopenhauer, The World as Will and Idea (trans. Haldane and Kepm), III, 107, 108.
124. E. von Hartmann : *Philosophy of the Unconscious* (trans. Coupland), II, 293, note.
125. Bergson : *Mind-Energy*, p. 25.
126. *Hartmann : op.cit.*, II, 330.
127. *E. Von Hartmann*, Philosophy of the unconscious (trans. Coupland) II, p. 330.
128. Ravaisson : "De l' habitude", Revue de métaphysique et de morale, XII (1894), 28.
129. A.A. Cournot, Essai sur les fondaments de nos connaissances (1851), Vol. I, paras. 285-86.
130. *Ibid.*, vol. I, para. 131.
131. A.A. Cournot, Essai sur les fondaments de nos connaissances (1851), Vol. I, paras 129-30.
132. Cournot : Traite de l'enchainement des idées fondamentalses dans les sciences et les arts (1861), Vol. I, para. 282.
133. *Ibid.*, para. 12.
134. Cournot, Essai, Vol. I, para. 66.
135. Bergson : *Creative Evolution*, p. 135.
136. 'This view of adaptation has been noted by M.F. Marin in a remarkable article on the origin of species' (*Creative Evolution*, p. 102, note).

137. Cournot also protested against rigid classification by species (Traité, Vol. I, para. 266). Bergson notices the difficulty of defining an individual (C.E., p. 12).
138. F. Marin : "Sur l'origine des espèces", Revue scientifique, 4th series, XVI (1901), p. 580.
139. *Ibid.*, p. 581. We note here that the development of identical organs in different environments proves the impulsion of the *élan*. Marin applied it to different individuals of the same species, Cournot, like Bergson, to individuals of highly divergent species.
140. Emile Durkheinm : *Elementary Forms of the Religious Life*, p. 16; Two sources, pp. 94-95. Bergson criticises Durkheim for ignoring individual psychology too much.
141. Emile Durkheim : *Elementary Forms of the Religious Life*, p. 16 : *Two sources*, pp. 17, 43, 47 (definition).
142. Bergson : *The two Sources of Morality and Religion*, pp. 6-7. Like Durkheim, Bergson recognises that our memory, imagination and language are society in us.
143. Bergson : *The two Sources of Morality and Religion*, pp. 15-17, 41, 190, 194 (definition), 7.
144. E. Durkheim, *The Elementary Forms of the Religious Life*, pp. 417, 425, 427 (quotation).
145. E. Durkheim, *The Elementary Forms of the Religious Life*, p. 428.
146. *Ibid.*, pp. 446-47.
147. J. Lachelier, Psychologie et metaphysique. Oeuvres, I, 198, 195.
148. A. Fouillée La Liberté et le determinisme (3rd ed.), p. 92.
149. Bergson, *Time and Free Will*, p. 172.
150. Augustin Guyau, La Philosophie et la sociologie d' Alfred Fouillée, p. 115.
151. Augustin Guyau, La Philosophie et la sociologie d' Alfred Fouillée, p. 116. On the evidence of *Creative Evolution*, Bergson means that the souls created have pre-existed in the élan vital (Creative Evolution, pp. 269-70).
152. "The mother beholding her child is joyous, because she is conscious of having created it, physically and morally...... If, then, in every domain the triumph of life is creation, must we not suppose that human life has its goal in a creation which, unlike that of the artist and philosopher, can be pursued always by all men—creation of self by self, the growing of the personality by an effort which draws much from little, something from nothing, and adds unceasingly to whatever wealth the world contains?" Bergson, "*Life and Consciousness*," *Mind-Energy*, pp. 29, 30-31.
153. J.M. Guyau, Esquisse d'une morale sans obligation ni sanction, p. 24.
154. J.M. Guyau, L' Irréligion de l'avenir, p. 470.
155. Bergson, *Creative Evolution*, p. 286.

156. A. Guyau, La Philosophie et la sociologie d' Alfred Fouillee, p. 116.
157. Compare Bergson's note on Plotinus, *Creative Evolution*, p. 210 : "The relation that we establish in the present chapter between 'extension' and 'detension' resembles in some aspects that which Plotinus supposes (some developments of which must have inspired M. Ravaisson) when he makes extension not indeed an inversion of original Being, but enfeeblement of its essence."
158. *The two Sources*, p. 210. The preceding quotations from Plotinus come from : i, 1, 2 (Ennead, Tractati, section); i, 1, 12; i, 4, 10; i, 4, 8; ii, 6, 7; v, 2, 1, and iii, 8, 9; iv, 4, 36; iv, 9, 3; i, 6, 7. They re from the first volume of Mc.Kennan's translation, i.e., the First Ennead and the Preller Ritter extracts.
159. Bergson, *The two Sources of Morality and Religion*, p. 216, note 2.

## *Chapter III*

# The Concept of God in Bergson's Philosophy

It is customary for any philosopher to put forward his philosophy with his own techniques and when he is put in certain difficulties in defending it, he seeks the concept of God. Bergson is not an exception to this. In his earlier work *The Creative Evolution* (1907), he conceives Reality in a scientific manner. His concept of vital impulse or élan vital is the blend of science and metaphysics. Even though, in this work he does not mention frequently about God, it is certain that by God, he means continuous creation, freedom and change. God, for him is actually not of the moral highest or the God of the theologians. Like the Absolute of philosophy or the God of religion, Bergson's Reality is Élan Vital. Whether he names it as Reality or God it is one and the same. But this God of Bergson is *change and impulsive.* The Élan Vital is the *source* of all creation and evolution. It is from the *back* that it acts as an impulse to create and change in duration. There seems to be no destiny or goal to reach, by this kind of evolution.

In 1932, Bergson's another important work *The two Sources of Morality and Religion* appeared. His notions about Reality changed considerably when this book was written by him. He made it plain in this work that he was favourably disposed toward Christianity. It is very interesting to note how he shifted his notion about Reality from an *impersonal push* to a *personal God.*

## 1. GOD AS IMPULSIVE

The simple formula through which we can construe Bergson's Reality is this :

Reality = Freedom = Change = Creation = God. This is cyclic and Élan Vital or the dynamic force is the Reality that Bergson conceives. In his *Time and Free Will* Bergson says that Reality is *'duration'*. Pure duration is nothing but uninterrupted flow and unimpeded movement. It cannot be measured; it cannot be represented by means of any diagram. All attempts to do so ends only by reducing Time to Space. It is not homogeneous, like Space. Unlike points in Space, no two moments of Time are alike. There cannot be any talk of the repetition of the same moments of time. Each moment is unique and irrepeatable. Irrepeatability and uniqueness are the chief characteristics of Reality. They are also the main features of freedom. A man's action cannot be predicted by others. Even with regard to one's own future actions, prediction is impossible. This is the kind of Reality Bergson speaks in his *Time and Free Will.*

In his *Creative Evolution,* he talks of a life force which is the cause of perpetual creation, perennial invention and continual novelty. The two features of such a kind of evolution are that the evolution has got (1) no source or (2) the source and the product are the same. Since God and Reality are the same, when talking about God Bergson says in this book." ........I speak of a centre from which worlds shoot out like rockets in a fire-works display-provided, however, that I do not present this centre as a *thing,* but as a continuity of shooting out. God, thus defined has nothing of the already made; He is unceasing life, action, freedom."[1] Here we must note that God is not spoken of as a *Being.* He is only a tendency. Let us see what Henri C. Corrance says about Bergson's concept of God : "Bergson's theory of God concerns only metaphysics. It does not touch the moral question at all..... Bergson's Creator is immanent in nature, but not, like the God of Pantheism, identical with it. He is continually trying to express himself under conditions which are more or less opposed to his freedom, and which he is only partially successful in overcoming. Yet he is ever 'making all things new' in a sense which is in direct contrast and contradiction to the static philosophy. He lives in duration, not in 'eternity', and, therefore, at least his liberty is not self-limited by any absolute finalist scheme. There is finalism in the universe, but it is in no sense rigid or determinate. It consists of the forward spring (élan) of the spiritual and life principle, by which it seeks, apparently to realize itself; though, like a winding river, it cannot go direct, but encounters many obstacles which divert it from its course. Thus, life is full of surprises and can never be anticipated, because no two moments are ever the same, but every new moment is coloured and qualified by the whole past which lives in it, and itself enters into and qualifies the past. The work of creation is ever proceeding, and Bergson's God is truly a living God."[2]

In *Creative Evolution*, Bergson maintains that he is against any sort of mysticism and his God is not the mystic's God. Regarding this he says, "If by mysticism be (as it almost always is nowadays) a reaction against positive science, the doctrine I defend is in the end only a protest against mysticism."[3] Of course, in his later work he changes this view and gives importance to mysticism. For Bergson the vital impetus is the ultimate Reality. It is both biological and metaphysical. Since we are concerned with Bergson's God as *impulsive,* we should elaborately discuss the biological history, nature, function and other essential characteristics of the *vital impulse* which Bergson introduces in his *Creative Evolution.* Here we must note that his description of life force (Élan Vital) is largely biased towards scientific side. He gives no room for any theological concepts such as God, soul, liberation etc. One can also see his philosophy of *'Becoming'* threading all through his descriptions of the vital impulse.

## The Vital Impulse

Before establishing his own theory of evolution in which the vital impulse is the main thing, Bergson has the duty of refuting the previous theories of evolution, both scientific and non-scientific. So, according to Bergson vitalism, mechanism, finalism and voluntarism are inadequate in one way or other. The scientific evolutionists such as Darwin, Weissmann and Lamarck are not also sailing in the same boat with Bergson in this regard. The important points to be noted in this section are : 1. That the past continues to survive in the present and thus we have *'duration'*; 2. That the evolution is creative and thus we have *creation*. By supposing one original impulse at the back of all, the theory of creative evolution can account for unity and harmony, and by supposing the spontaneous disruption of the same principle it can also account for novelty, diversity and discord.

## Organised and Unorganised Bodies

When we view the universe from the psychological standpoint we can see that our activity is the central fact. Consciousness plays on the zone of our activity and it is a tension which holds the past in the present experience. The mind is confined to our consciousness, if not to our body; but the body which is the centre of our activity has a beginning and an end. We do not know its absolute beginning. ".....It arises from a germ that carries within it the accumulated past of an indefinitely long ancestry, and it has no absolute end, for it passes on this current of life to a new generation of germs."[4] The more we question about the mystery of life, the more we have to study the relation of mind and body. Our bodily existence with mind, the external world and our perception of objects have got many more things to tell us. The organised bodies with consciousness, the brain which is the wonderful material organism and the relation that the organised body has got between its brain and mind has also to be found out. Certain intelligent activities reveal to us that mind cannot be the product of the brain...... "The brain is a motor mechanism, an organism for the reception and trans-mission of movement, and the instrument of the mind whose reality it neither creates nor maintains."[5]

If we ask what life is, it seems to us that is a power or property or function that some objects possess of organising themselves. Their organisation with particular characteristics give them individual bodies. Organised bodies make use of the unorganised bodies for their support and reproduction. As we study these living bodies we can note that there is something in which the phenomenon of life alone is present which passes on the life it holds from one generation to another. "Continuity of change, preservation of the past in the present, real duration—the living being seems, then, to share these attributes with consciousness. Can we go further and say that life, like conscious activity, is invention, in unceasing creation?"[6] According to Weismannism : "Life is a current passing from germ to germ through the medium of a developed organism. There is a continuous and invisible progress like that of a consciousness."[7] Modern science says that the substance which contains within it the whole of that reality which has developed innumerable forms is *protoplasm*. But the process of reproduction and the whole phenomenon of life in this planet is simple in its origin and continuous in its development. "......Life is a reality that overflows matter, that matter, protoplasm, is to it what the body is to the mind, the instrument which it has formed to do its work."[8]

## Mechanism and Vitalism

There are two scientific theories of life : *mechanism* and *vitalism*. Their controversies are inevitable since both these are scientific theorie. All the phenomena of living matter, according to the scientific theory are a combination of purely material elements. Whatever may be the constitution of matter we cannot differentiate between a living and non-living matter. The living matter is only the complex structure of unorganised matter. Living matter and its various processes—growth, nutrition, assimilation and reproduction—are all of the same ultimate nature as the grouping of molecules in the unorganised non-living material elements. Just like the material elements have attraction, repulsion etc., the living-matter has got its own processes. Protoplasm which is the source of all living processes would have attained its power by the combination of material elements. The protoplasm can also be analysed by human intellect like other material elements.

Mechanism means that nothing new comes out of the universe, nothing that is not already there. All changes are reversible though not practically. Mechanistic principle is directly applicable to science and it is accepted in all the physical sciences as an axiom. Any limits which we might have to set to its universality are practically negligible. But when we apply the mechanistic theory to natural science especially to biology we have the difficulties. In biology we have the life which gives more in the result than is present in the conditions. The axiom of mechanistic theory when applied to physical science finds no such difficulty as we encounter in biology. There is contradiction of this axiom in biological science. Life is most apparent in lowly organisms and when we consider vital phenomena in their simplest manifestations because here the vital movements closely resemble physical movements and some physical movements approach so closely to vital movements. So, it is difficult to say that if there is any impassable gulf between these two movements.

### Mechanism and Finalism

But the above mentioned difficulties become serious when we observe the movements of the most developed organisms since we note the significant changes between the physical and the vital movements in the developed living beings. There are certain facts of biology which cannot be included in mechanistic theory and so a theory just opposite of this was formulated indicating a destiny towards which the vital movements are directed. This theory is called *finalism* since it emphasises the existence of a principle, the very reverse of mechanism which finds all explanation in the past, a principle which indicates a purpose to be fulfilled in the future. Bergson refutes both mechanism and finalism (teleology) on the grounds that the first proceeds on the causal theory that "the same causes produce the same effects" or for the first theory 'all is given'; in short it is the realization of a pre-designed plan whereas the second emphasises the *order* and goal; in short it is a *reversed mechanism* because it is also realizing a pre-designed plan. As Bergson says, "That two walkers starting from different points and wandering at random should finally meet, is no wonder. But that, throughout their walk, they should describe two indentical curves exactly superposable on each other, is altogether unlikely. The improbability will be the greater, the more complicated the routes; and it will become impossibility, if the zigzags are infinitely complicated. Now, what is this complexity of zigzags as compared with that of an organ in which thousands of different cells, each being itself a kind of organism, are arranged in a definite order."[9] The above facts led some natural scientists to formulate the theory of vitalism.

**Vitalism is 'Purposive'**

Vitalism describes a philosophical theory. Bergson uses this term because for him life is the ultimate reality and as a philosophical theory it contrasts rationalism with voluntarism. Rationalism gives priority to intellectual knowledge or reason whereas voluntarism gives priority to conation or will. Here we use the term vitalism to denote scientific theory only. There are certain vital phenomena which cannot be explained as resulting from the conditions present in the immediately preceding state as mechanism implies. In vital activity we see an entirely new principle at work. We see purpose in vital activity which directs the activity to an end that is realizable in future. If mechanism were true then every state of a living cell must be wholly conditioned by the previous state. The present condition of the environment also affects the living cell. But we find something quite different. We find that in plants, animals and in some other living beings, there is something which regulates the work of the different parts of the organism purely with regard to the well-being of the organism as a whole. "Thus, if we injure an organ, cells whose ordinary function is quite different will take on the duty of forming repairing tissue. If a newt loses a limb, cells which were performing quite different work will restore the limb, making it the exact counterpart of the lost limb, or rather will restore the animal to what it would have been if it had not suffered the loss. Professor Driesch in a famous experiment has shown that if we divide the embryo of a sea-urchin we can get cells which normally would have produced special parts of an individual sea-urchin to develop into complete individual sea-urchins. We can in fact separate the cells at the stage of the second subdivision of the nucleus and obtain four individuals in place of the one. These facts show that in a living organism the life principle acts with regard to the whole and directs and controls the parts strictly with regard to the purpose and function of the whole."[10]

### Entelechy and Problem of Evolution

The vitalists maintain that life is of the nature of an *entelechy,* using the Aristotelian word. Human ovum and spermatozoan are minute masses of protoplasm. Yet the entelechy of each and their union contain the direction and variety of functions to impose at every stage of development of the structure even though the tissue is very minute. If we maintain that each tissue has got its own entelechy there are as many entelechies as there are tissues in our body. The difficulty arises when we have an entelechy of our body as a whole apart from the individual cells of our body. Complete individuality cannot therefore be maintained. If each cell has an entelechy, then what is the relation of each to the entelechy that constitutes the whole body? We are remedied here of Leibniz's *windowless monads,* "simple substances into which and out of which nothing can pass, but each of which is a self-centred individual experience in harmony with other centres, within a universe reflected in each." But Leibniz invoked the conception of God and supposed a pre-established harmony imposed by His direct act between the individual monad with the general harmony of the whole. Like Leibniz the vitalist has no such pre-established harmony and hence the problem remains to be solved.

Evolution poses many more problems which neither mechanism nor vitalism can explain. The history of living forms reveal to us two facts. One is that every individual living being has got an absolutely continuous past. This is the continuity of an indefinite past in a living present. It is not produced by but carries along with it the continuous past. What we see in the living beings are not merely the kaleidoscopic groupings of atoms. The other fact is the transformism. Transformation takes place according to the altered conditions of the environment and this change whether it is regular or spasmodic in its periodicity, is the origin of species. The former is the *duration* of living forms, and the latter is the creation of new forms.

### Darwin, Weissmann and Lamarck

There are two opposed theories of evolution. One is Darwin's theory of Natural Selection. According to this theory the individual efforts of the living begins have got no account in their survival. Circumstances beyond their control have eliminated the unfit and allowed the fittest to survive. This theory has been emphasized in Weissmann's hypothesis of the continuity of germ-plasm according to which only the somatic cells which form the body of the individual and which alone undergo development or acquire character during the life of the individual undergo change. The germs containing the vital characters of the individual do not change. So, the struggle for existence is ultimately a struggle of the germs and not of the individuals. The second theory is the older Lamarckian theory according to which 'the variation which results in a new species is not an accidental variation inherent in the germ, but springs from the effort of the living creature itself as to adapt itself to the circumstances of its existence.'[11] Neo-Lamarckian theory emphasises consciousness and will in the effort and so this is a psychological and internal principle of development.

**Creative Evolution**

In the above principles even though there are truths, they are not sufficient to explain fully the great facts of evolution. From the present activity of a living being the whole of its activity cannot be known. The protoplasm cannot give us the *duration* and *creation*. Evolution has to be conceived as a continous movement which manifests itself in the individual forms it produces. "*It is a movement the form of whose activity is shown in its tendency to concentrate and contract into a tension, in its turn to be relaxed in an extension, the type of which activity we each experience in our own life which is very part of it. This conception is Bergson's doctrine of the vital impulse,—the spring of life, and the principle that explains it he has named creative evolution.*"[12]

**Brain and Memory**

If we apprehend the nature of *memory*, the ideas of duration and creation will be clear. In every activity of our life we are compelled to recognise that the whole past is functioning in a present movement. Our body has sensory and motor organs and brain is the central organ. "The sensory mechanism simply receives and transmits external influence to the brain which, acting as a central telephone exchange," directs the energy either along a special motor path, or arrests it and breaks it up to be distributed among all the motor centres. Bergson say that if we accept the materialistic conception of memory we cannot give satisfactory explanation to the problem of how from unconscious impressions in the brain conscious *memory could at all arise.* His hypothesis has no such difficulty because for him whatever happens is conserved by the basic Reality in us. Memory is the selective application of past experience to present action. Our brain is an instrument of selection. With the help of our brain we recall or get out of our past experience conserved in Reality, the part is of practical use at the moment. *The brain is a selector rather than a generator.* "Such is the brain's part in the work of memory : it does not serve to preserve the past, but primarily to mark it, then to allow what is practically useful to emerge through the mask".[13] Our brain is the organ of attention to practical life. "It is only the mechanisation of recall, and not a store of ideas. It simply stores motor habits."[14]

**Life and Duration**

Life is something that endures. It is a time existence, something that endures and changes continually, endures by changing, in that it carries with it all its past into its present activity. So, for Bergson memory or consciousness is the basic Reality. Consciousness "signifies, before everything, memory."[15] Bergson's concept of Time or Duration involves the idea of conservation of the entire past and its penetration into the present. "So, to say that Reality is conscious is but another way of saying that it endures and preserves the past."[16] Consciousness or memory not only retains the past but also creates and anticipates future. "To retain what no longer is, to anticipate what as yet is not—there are the primary functions of consciousness."[17] Hence, Reality is conscious both because of its conservation of the past and its creation of the future.

### Evolution is Continuous and Unforeseeable

Creation cannot be adequately explained either by mechanism or vitalism. It is due to the fact that it is *continuous* and *unforeseeable* in nature. In a machine we see that each part plays its role to run it and the machine as a whole is the association of so many parts. There is nothing more in the whole than is present in its parts. But in an organism it is different and it is reverse. Only our intellect finds different parts in an organism which are so arranged that the organism maintains its stability and harmony with its parts. Actually in an organism there are no parts having separate existence of their own. The more we study the structure of an organism, the more we are lost in wonder at the complexity of the parts. Paley in his *Natural Theology* uses this as a theistic argument stating that only a divine artificer of infinite intelligence and power could have assembled and designed that machine which is the living body. An organism lives and grows by continual creation and the whole is prior to its parts. Each moment something new is created and nothing repeats itself. What is true of each organism is true of the evolution of life generally. Life is not created by protoplasm. Protoplasm is used by life as an instrument. By means of developed organism the original impulse is passing from generation to generation of germs. Life, or the vital impulse consists in a demand for creation. It is 'a will to create.' In the passing from one germ to another through the medium of a developed organism we see an internal push that has carried life by more and more complex forms to higher and higher destinies. It is a dynamic continuity of qualitative progress. The 'duration' leaves its bite on things. The evolutionary process is progressive.

### Evolution does not take Place in Straight Line

The impetus splits up more and more. Life, in proportion to its progress, is scattered in manifestations which undoubtedly owe to their common origin the fact that they are complementary to each other in certain aspects. They are nonetheless mutually incompatible and antagonistic. The discord between species will go on increasing. "There are species which are arrested, there are some that retrogress. Evolution is not only a movement forward; in many cases we observe a marking-time, and still more often a deviation or turning back. Thence results an increasing disorder. No doubt there is progress, if progress means a continual advance in the general direction determined by a first impulsion; but this progress is accomplished only on the two or three great lines of Evolution on which forms ever more and more complex, ever more and more high, appear; between these lines run a crowd of minor paths in which deviations, arrests, and set-backs are multiplied."[18] The spring of our vital activity lies in the vital impulse that lies behind us. This impulse is a *tendency*. As this tendency progresses we see the divergent paths of one and the same vital impulse.

### Bergson and Aristotle

What Bergson says as the three major divisions of the vital impulse namely the plants, the animals and the man are *the divisions of kind and not of degree.* But Aristotle says that the difference between the above three is *one of degree and not of kind.* For Aristotle the evolution is a logical process and not a time process. But for Bergson evolution takes place in time (duration). In Aristotle's theory of evolution the lower contains the higher potentially and thus maintaining the difference between the developments of evolution as one of degree. "The process involved is not a time-process, it is a logical process, and the development is a logical development. The lower always contains the higher potentially. The man is in the ape ideally. The higher, again, contains the lower actually. The man is all that the ape is, and more also. What is merely implicit in the lower form is explicit in the higher. The form which is dimly seen struggling to light in the lower, has realised itself in the higher. The higher is the same thing as the lower, but it is the same thing in a more evolved state. The higher presupposes the lower and rests upon it as foundation. The higher is the form of which the lower is the matter. It actually is what the lower is struggling to become. Hence, the entire universe is one continuous chain. It is a process; not a time process, but an eternal process."[19]

## Vital Impulse is the Common Origin to both Matter and Life

In spite of divergent paths and developments the vital impulse retains and imparts what belongs to its common origin. Here we are confronted with a problem analogous to that body. Life is continuous development and matter is a resisting force which retards the progress of life. Our actions are realized only in our body which the mind uses as an instrument. The theory that body is prior to mind is as false as to say that matter is prior to life. Life is duration and matter is a limit. A limit cannot contain with it, and be prior to the whole which is limitless. So, matter cannot be prior to life. It is just like saying that space is prior to time if we say that matter is prior to life.

## Instinct and Intelligence

We can go on mentioning the problems of evolution. It is sufficient here if we mention one feature of human evolution. It is our mental activity which has two distinct modes—*instinct* and *intelligence.* "The twofold form of consciousness, intuition and intelligene, is due to the twofold form of the real, life and matter. Intuition is the knowledge of life, intelligence is the knowledge of matter. Intuition is instinct, sympathy, an apprehension of reality from within. It is the artist's insight. It is the lover's devotion, the mother's sacrifice. It is all in our consciousness which enters into the feeling that our life continues itself in the reality which it apprehends. Intelligence on the contrary is the knowledge of a reality as we view it externally, the apprehension of that which stands over against us, it may be opposing us. It is the taking stock of our situation. Instinct is innate knowledge. Intelligence is acquired knowledge."[20]

Since instinct and intelligence are the two modes of activity opposed to each other in all respects they are different in kind. They are not identical, but complementary. Both instinct and intelligence have opposed directions. "Instinct is not degraded intelligence, and intelligence is not uplifted instinct."[21] Instinct attained its perfection in the invertebrates culminating in the insect hymenoptera and intelligence attained its perfection in the vertebrates culminating in man. So, we can see clearly that in the one line of evolution there is intellect and in the another there is instinct. Nowhere can we see intelligence evolving into instinct and vice versa.

**Intellect and Matter**

What, then, is really intellect? How it is distinguished from instinct? The answer is that intellect gives us the knowledge of matter. Nature itself has got no outlines. It is only our intellect based upon our actions outlines nature. The world is continuous with the universe. Our limiting knowledge by its static nature separates the whole into discontinuous outlines for convenience. Intellect has not come into being ready made. Both intellect and matter have progressed in course of evolution and these two cannot be unconnected. The evolution of the one involves the evolution of the other. The intellect is the mode of apprehending reality as matter, and matter becomes more and more fixed into definite stable things with clear outlines as the intellect develops its power to use it. This is what we call as the correlation between the intellect as a mode of apprehending and matter as the order in which reality is apprehended.

This method of correlating differs from philosophical doctrine since this correlation is from the standpoint of action and not from the standpoint of knowledge. From the nature of intelligence and instinct we understand that matter is the condition of life. In mind and body relation we have seen that though body is the condition for our mental activities, mind overflows the body and body is used by mind only as an instrument of action. In the same way we have the life overflowing matter and matter being used by life as an instrument for further progress. Life manifests itself in material forms and matter is continuous with those forms giving shape to life's activities. It is as false to say that only matter is the ultimate reality as saying that only life is the ultimate reality. We must establish the reality of both. According to Bergson both life and matter are the two aspects of one and the same reality *i.e.*, the vital impulse. Both of them are opposed in tendencies, but complementing each other. We do not understand the nature of life through our scientific knowledge. The more science advances, the more life recedes. The more our intellect materialises life, the more is matter spatialised. The mobility of life cannot be fixed by intellect's stable and immobile concepts. If the intellect attempts to study by its static concepts the dynamic reality it drifts away from it.

**Life Impulse is a Tension**

So, to sum up the above discussion regarding Bergson's concept of vital impulse we can say the following :

Life impulse is a tension. The past with its inexhaustible qualities acts on the present. Even though there are multiplicity of qualities, they interpenetrate and they do not lie outside one another. The tension of the vital impulse is interrupted by the extension of matter. Extension of matter is the movement in the inverse direction. The tension, when interrupted spreads and all the characters and qualities are let go since the spring is released. In the unrolling of the vital impulse, its qualities and characters no longer permeate in an unextended point. Bergson's metaphysical principle lies in the extension of the original tension of the interrupted vital impulse.

The lengthy discussion above will reveal how Bergson conceives the vital impulse as Reality. This Reality is a tendency and it is also spoken of as God by Bergson. His knowledge of science combined with metaphysics had shaped a Reality of the kind we have seen which acts as an *impersonal push* which is the cause for all changes that take place. Change is unceasing. This *impersonal push* can be compared to *"tṛṣṇā"* of Buddhistic philosophy. But an important difference between Buddhistic theory of change and Bergson's theory of change is this : For Bergson error lies in our conceiving the *One* as *many* static units. But for Buddhistic theory, error lies in conceiving the many static units as the *"One comprehensive whole."*

## 2. CHANGE

From the earliest times recorded in the history of philosophy, philosophers have never stopped saying that everything changes : We have in the West Heraclitus, Zeno, Plato, Aristotle, Descartes, Spinoza, Leibniz and Kant advocate this view. In the East, the Buddhistic doctrine of Kṣaṇika Vāda of Indian Philosophy, the Confucian and Taoist theories of change in the Chinese Philosophy are all referring to this kind of philosophy. But what is the speciality we have in Bergson's philosophy of change? *Change* is fundamental in his philosophy. In fact for Bergson Reality or God (for our purpose) itself is change. The mathematical and physical sciences help him to put forward his philosophy of change in his own way. The vital impulse acts from the back to create novel things. But without change there is no creation. So, the principle of change and vital impulse are not fundamentally different, though for our convenience we treat them separately. We shall now see the nature of the problem of change and Bergson's explanation of it.

### Two kinds of Change

1. "His theory of change which discusses change as a cosmic principle, which Bergson calls élan vital.

2. Bergson's theory of change when regarded as the principle working within the individual, which Bergson calls duration.'[22] Bergson founded his philosophy of change after refuting the theories of change of his predecessors (namely Zeno, Plato, Aristotle, Descartes, Spinoza, Leibniz and Kant). The one sided emphasis of the rationalists and the empiricists on the unity and the multiplicity are refuted by Bergson. According to him change is an indivisible flow of duration. When regarded as an antinomical concept change becomes a philosophical problem. The solution must therefore be to grasp change not intellectually as an antinomical concept, but intuitively as an indivisible flow of duration.

## The Nature of the Problem of Change

### *Change Implies Time*

When we say, 'A changes'—the statement implies that 'A is in time', because to be changing means to be in time. Therefore, it is necessary to understand the nature of change. What is time? Is it succession or is it duration? It cannot be succession because succession is regarded to take place in time. It cannot be duration because events endure in time. This implies that time is the receptacle for succession and duration to take place. This means that such a kind of time is static and permanent. Here, it does not have the characteristic of transcience.

Is time the three-fold division of past, present and future? No. Because this is a temporal division. This division takes place in time. It presupposes time. The present is that which is occurring. The past is that which has ceased to occur and the future is that which is yet to occur. To understand the past as past and the future as future we must know the nature of present because only with reference to the present, the past is intelligible as past and the future is intelligible as future. But present cannot be described in terms of past or future. Our perception takes place in one of the three modes of past, present and future. But the strict present is dynamic by nature. It is a shifting present and so, we have many successive presents. We cannot know them as succession because we ourselves must be above succession which is impossible. The relation between the future and the present is not possible. Because the future is that which is yet to come into being and the present is that which is existing. Similar is the case regarding the relation between the present and the past. But to understand time we have to divide it into the past, the present and the future. If we divide time in this manner our attempt to relate them creates a contradictory situation. By nature, time is transcient and so the divisions are impossible to unite. Moreover, the attempt to unite them makes time permanent, with the result that time ceases to be time.

### *Change and Causality*

Time implies change which, in turn, refers to causality. An object has a cause for its existence and this means that it has a sufficient ground for its existence. That is, its present existence is anticipated in the past. It is not entirely a new product. "The causality is therefore not a bare succession of discrete phenomena, but the existence of a self-transcending thing (self-transcending in the sense that it can be intelligible only in the light of its development in the past). For instance when ice melts into water, or when milk turns into curd, we believe that there is a continuity between these phenomena—a continuity, which makes it a continuous process and not a contingent succession. In other words, we believe in a continuity underlying the processes that enable us to say in each case, that it is the same (identical) substance which appears in a different form."[23] Everything transcends itself and has something else as its cause. The other thing, in turn, has some third thing as its cause. It also is incomplete and imperfect. So, it transcends itself by relating itself with other things. This chain of cause and effect leads to the infinite regress. This can only be avoided by our belief in a Prime or an *uncaused cause* with reference to which, all the other relations (of the chain) are regarded as the effects without itself being an effect of any cause other than itself. This line of reasoning points to a cause, which being timeless ceases to be a cause.

## Bergson's Treatment of the Problem of Change

**Intellect cannot grasp change :** Bergson establishes his theory of change after criticising his predecessors (namely Zeno, Plato, Aristotle, Descartes, Spinoza, Leibniz and Kant). Bergson thinks that philosophy, which begins with Plato and ends with Plotinus, is the development of the following principle : "There is more in the immutable than in the moving, and one passes from the stable to the unstable by a single diminution."[24] The main reason why we are not able to grasp the reality of continuous change is owing to the limitations of our intellectual nature. "We are made in order to act, as much as and more than in order to think—or, rather, when we follow the bent of our nature, it is in order to act that we think."[25] Intellect always tries to carve out for itself stable forms because it is primarily fitted for action, and "is characterized by a natural inability to comprehend life" and grasp change.[26]

**Duration is continuous flow :** Self is duration. It can only be directly grasped by intuition. When I say that 'I change' the change seems to me in the passage from one stage to the next. During all the time of its existence it remains the same (unchanged) if we take each of these states separately. But there is no feeling, no idea, no will—which does not undergo change at every moment. If a mental state ceases to vary (change), its duration ceases to flow. For instance, in the visual perception of a motionless, external object inspite of the fact that the object remains the same and although I may look at it from the same side and from the same angle, in the same light, the visual perception that I have of the object, differs from that which I have just had. One may be an instant older than the other. My memory, which is present there conveys to me something of the past into the present. Similar is the case regarding the more deeply internal states, such as the sensations, feelings, etc., which do not correspond to a simple visual perception directly. We regard these internal states changing, whenever there is noticeable change. Whereas 'the truth is that we change without ceasing and that the state itself is nothing but change.'[27]

This amounts to saying that there is no essential difference between passing from one state to another and persisting in the same state.[28] Because we do not take notice of the continuous change of every psychic state, we speak as if a new state were placed alongside the previous one (juxtaposed in space). We think that the new state is not subject to change. (Similarly, we think of every new state which is born). Thus, 'the apparent discontinuity of the psychical life is then due to our attention being fixed on it by a series of separate acts : actually there is only a gentle slope; but in following the broken line of our acts of attention, we think we perceive separate steps.'[29]

**Psychic states are not psychic life :** According to Bergson, our psychic life, is full of the unseen. The incidents seem to be cut off from those which precede as well as those which succeed them. Though they appear to be discontinuous, they in fact stand out against the continuity of a background on which they are designed. Our attention is directed towards them, because they interest us more. 'But each of them is borne by the fluid mass of our whole psychical existence. Each is only the best illuminated point of a moving zone which comprises all that we feel or think or will—all, in short that we are at any given moment. It is this entire zone which in reality makes up our state. Now, states thus defined cannot be regarded as distinct elements. They continue each other in an endless flow. Our attention perceives them as distinct, solid states separate from one another and reunites artificialy.

The flux of fleeting states is a colourless substratum. It is coloured by psychic states which cover it. We perceive only what is coloured. 'As a matter of fact, this substratum has no reality, it is merely a symbol intended to recall unceasingly to our consciousness the artificial character of the process by which the attention places cleanout states side by side, where actually there is a continuity which unfolds.'[30]

**Survival of the Past in the Present**

We think that our existence is composed of separate states with an unchanging ego as its underlying substratum. Therefore, we have a wrong belief that there is no duration. This is because of our thinking that an ego does not endure since it does not change. By eliminating the real time we get an artificial imitation of internal life. This is presented as its static equivalent. But, if we eliminate the symbol concealing what Bergson calls psychic life, we find that time is just the stuff of which they are made. "Our duration is not merely one instant replacing another, if it were, there would never be anything but the present—no prolonging of the past into the actual, no evolution, no concrete duration."[31] Duration is the continuous progress of the past which gnaws into the future and which swells as it advances. And as the past grows without ceasing, so also there is no limit to its preservation. Memory, as we have tried to prove,[32] is not a faculty of putting away recollections in a drawer, or of inscribing them in a register. There is no register, no drawer, there is not even, properly speaking, a faculty, for a faculty works intermittently when it will or when it can, whilst the piling up of the past upon the past goes on without relaxation. In reality, the past is preserved by itself automatically. In its entirety, probably, it follows us at every instant; 'all that we have felt, thought and willed from our earliest infancy is there, leaning over the present which is about to join it, pressing against the portals of consciousness that would fain leave it outside.'[33]

Our brain serves our practical purpose and it is constituted in that way. Through our memories we feel vaguely that our past remains present to us. We think with only a small part of our past. But it is with our entire past, including the original bent of our soul, that we desire, will and act. Our past is made manifest to us in its impulse. It is felt in the form of tendency, although only a small part of it only is known in the form of idea. From the survival of the past on the present we understand that our consciousness cannot go through the same state twice. "The circumstances may still be the same, but they will act no longer on the same person, since they find him at a new moment of his history. Our personality which is being built up each instant with its accumulated experience, changes without ceasing. By changing, it prevents any state, although superficially identical with another, from ever repeating it in its very depth. That is why our duration is irreversible. We could not live over again a single moment, for we should have to begin by effacing the memory of all that had followed. Even could we erase this memory from our intellect, we could not from our will."[34]

Thus our personality shoots, grows and ripens without ceasing. Each of its moments is something new added to what was before. We may go further : 'it is not only something new, but something unforeseeable.'[35]

"Doubtless my present state is explained by what was in me and by what was acting on me a moment ago. In analysing it I should find no other elements."[36]

Each of our states modifies our personality. It is therefore right to say that what we do, depends on what we are. But it is necessary to add also that what we are to a certain extent, is in accordance with (or, it depends upon) what we do. We are creating ourselves continually. This creation of self by self is found more complete, as the more one reasons on what one does.

### Movement or Change is Indivisible

For Bergson all change or movement is indivisible. The movement is unique and cannot be decomposed. We picture to ourselves that the movement is infinitely divisible. This is due to the fact that the passage is made in space and the space is infinitely divisible. For the purposes of action and of practical life we are in need of static points to represent original movement. The immobility is convenient to our senses. Though for all our practical purposes we require the notion of immobility as part of our mental equipment, it does not at all help us to grasp reality. Then it is regarded by us that movement is something superadded to the motionless. For the world of affairs this is quite legitimate. But when we bring this habit into the world of speculation, we misconceive reality. We create insoluble problems. All true change or movement is indivisible. By constructing fictitious states and trying to compose movement out of them, we endeavour to make a process coincide with a thing—a movement with an immobility. If movement is not everything, it is nothing. If we postulate that the motionless is real, then we shall be incapable of grasping reality.

### Intellect and Matter are Opposed to Life

Our intellect loves the solid and the static, but life itself is not static—it is dynamic. It takes views across the ever—moving scene, snapshots of reality. It acts like the camera of the cinematograph operator, which is capable of producing only photographs. The photographs are successive and static, in a series upon a ribbon. In order to grasp reality, we have to do what the cinematograph does with the film—that is, introduce or rather, re-introduce movement.[37] The still photograph is an abstraction bereft of movement. So, also our intellectual views of the world and of our own nature are static instead of being dynamic. Human life is not made up of childhood, adolescence, manhood, and old age as 'states.' Life is not a thing. It is not a state of a thing—it is a continuous movement or change. The soul itself is a movement, not an entity.

Even physical science does not assert now the fixity and the rigidity of matter. The researches of Einstein culminating in the formulation of his general Theory of Relativity and his special Theory of Gravitation threaten very seriously the older static views of the universe.[38]

### *Change is Absolute*

For Bergson, the reality of change is absolute. In connection with his study of Memory, he discusses Real Time (la duree), Freedom and Creative Evolution. He also says that universal 'becoming' is a vision of the reality of change. Then we can realize that change is substantial. It constitutes the very stuff of life. "There are changes, but there are not things that change; change does not need a support. There are movements, but there are not, necessarily, constant objects which are moved; movement does not imply something that is movable.'[39] We must conceive reality as a continuous flux. Then immobility will seem a superficial abstraction. If the Reality is change, then states, concepts, and substances will vanish. Apart from change there is no reality. All is movement. We ourselves are movement—part of an *élan,* which carries with it all things and all creatures, and that in this eternity—not of immutability but of life and change—"We live and move and have our being."[40]

Thus, we see that the vital impulse and the principle of change are interconnected. Bergson's theory of creative evolution anticipates the basic contention of the theory of emergent evolution namely that the process of evolution gives birth to *new* forms of existence. There are also notable differences between Bergson's creative evolution and emergent evolution. While emergent evolution is *inter-relation* of the many basic elements in new ways, creative evolution consists in the birth of the many new forms by the *diversification* of the one basic creative energy. Again, whereas emergent evolution places God at the end of the process, creative evolution puts God at the beginning, identifying it with the original impulse that drives the world from behind.

## 3. GOD AS LOVE AND CREATION

### (In the two Sources of Morality and Religion)

We have already seen the nature of God in *Creative Evolution*. In this work Bergson establishes that Reality is change. Change is Freedom. Freedom is to go on creating unceasingly. Creation is God. This kind of definition for God does not present before us any *personal God*. "The philosophy of change does not then sound any clear and confident note as to what lies beyond us in the unseen world. It does not present to us God as the loving father of the human race, whom He has begotten or created that intelligent beings may recognise Him and find happiness in communion with Him. There may be truth in this ideal, but it is no part of philosophy. Neither does it teach us the brotherhood of the human race."[41]

In his letter to *Father de Tonquedec Bergson writes :* 'I speak of God as the source whence issue successively, by an effort of his freedom, the currents of impulses each of which will make a world.'[42] Here, he clearly admits that the creative *'élan'* is not bereft of any centrality, but definitely issues forth from God. The source of evolution is God. But even now, Bergson does not admit the end of evolution. The logical consequence of it compels Bergson to admit that change is not the final word. Only in *The two Sources,* that Bergson frequently admits that the *'élan'* vital must terminate in God. He calls here the vital impulse as the impetus of Love that 'lifts humanity upto God and completes the divine creation.'[43]

Thus in the two Sources, we see that Bergson admits at last that the origin and the end of the creative *'élan'* is God. This is an outcome of his realization of the defects of his philosophy. Here, he 'arrives at a notion of *One Being* from whom the impetus of creativity takes its start. The individual souls and matter are creations out of the vital impulse.'[44] When speaking at the *Edinburgh Philosophical Society* in 1914, Bergson remarked that 'God is the creator of Creators.' The statement at that time was vague. His explanation about this became clear only when his last work was published in 1932.

### God must be experienced and not merely be known

We look upon an object as existing if it is perceived. Such an object is therefore presented in our experience. We must construct the idea of an object or of a being, as the geometrician does for a geometrical figure; but only experience can decide whether an object exists outside the idea thus constructed. The problem before us is whether there is a Being distinct from all other beings. Is that Being beyond our reach of experience, but yet exists like all other beings? If we answer this question in the affirmative, then we must prove that such a Being is indeed God. Philosophers never fail to attribute this Being with qualities. But all their attempts misfired because when they began to refer to that Being by attributes, it referred to some other thing. God should step down into our field of experience; Otherwise the concept of God attributed will have no meaning because such a God is not practical. Regarding this, Bergson says, 'For religion, be it static or dynamic, regards Him, above all, as a Being who can hold communication with us.'[45]

### Bergson's Refutation of the God of Plato and Aristotle

### Plato and the Idea of Good

For a long time, Platonic theory of Ideas dominated the Greek world. Aristotle's conception of the relation between the first principle and the world is the same as that between Idea and the thing of Plato. Ideas are the products of social and individual intelligence. There are relations between the immutable ideas and immutable things. But since it is possible to control our ideas, we cannot come to a conclusion that there are ideas for all the things in the world : There are possibilities for actual things to elude our grasp. Plato places above the world of senses a hierarchy of Ideas. At its apex we have the Idea of Ideas, which is the Idea of Good. For Bergson, since God must be experienced, an imaginary God of Plato is not acceptable.

## Bergson's Refutation of Aristotle's Conception of God

The God of Aristotle has nothing in common with the gods worshipped by the Greeks and the God of the Bible, or God of the Gospels. Aristotle talks of an *unmoved mover.* 'A given motion in the universe is produced by some other motion, this motion by a third motion and so on, and since an infinite regress is impossible, it is necessary that there should be, as the first cause of the series of motions, an unmoved mover or God. If the first cause of motion were itself in motion it would have to be moved by something else that moves, and so on ad infinitum, and this would leave motion unexplained. Somewhere, motion must begin without being caused by something that moves. Hence, there must be an eternal unmoved first mover, who is the final ground of all vital forces in nature.'[46]

Bergson disagrees with Aristotle when the latter says that 'God is thought-thinking-thought.' 'Thought alone of all human activities is ascribable to God. It is the highest function of man, the one trait of man which is truly divine. Man's reason is conceived as a spark of the divine reason. But what is the object of God's thought? Obviously, the only worthy object is God Himself; it is in this sense that God is describable as thought-thinking-though.'[47] In Aristotle's own words, ".......it must be itself that thought-thinks, and its thinking is a thinking on thinking." Man's thought differs from that of God. The former is discursive, that is, it proceeds in step-by-step from premise to conclusion; God's thought is entirely intuitive, that is, it grasp in a single flash of insight.

According to Bergson Aristotle's conception of Deity

"consists in deifying both the social work which paves the way for language and the individual constructive work requiring patterns and models : the Âld OS (Idea or Form) is what corresponds to this twofold work; the Idea of Ideas or Thought of Thoughts is therefore Divinity itself."[48] For Bergson, God as specified by Aristotle is inadequate; since by stating that God is the Idea of Ideas or Thought of Thoughts, it is inevitable to conceive these ideas standing for a stationary property or a state culled from some stage or other in the process of becoming. Reality is mobility. By having ideas, we have only to perceive continuties of change. To have any action on the real and 'to perform the constructive task which is the natural object of human intelligence, we must contrive to have halts here and there just as we wait for a momentary slowing down or standing still before firing at moving target.'[49] These halts are really simultaneousness of two or more movements; but not as they seem to be the suppression of movements. Since these snapshots of movement concern our action on things, rest is considered as something superior to movement. "Thus immobility is rated higher than mutability, which implies a deficiency, a lack, a quest of the unchanging form. Nay more, it is by this gap between the point where a thing is and the point where it should be, where it aspires to be, that movement and change will be defined and even measured. On this showing, duration becomes a debasement of being, time a deprivation of eternity. This whole system of metaphysics is involved in the Aristotelian conception of Deity".[50] Bergson, though refutes Aristotle's God as immobile, he himself becomes a victim of the same deficiency when he favours Christianity in *The two Sources.*

## God is Love and Creation

Since Aristotle's conception of God creates insoluble problems, Bergson says that God must be experienced through mysticism. Love and Creation are God Himself. The object of mysticism is God. In Bergson's own words, "God is love, and the object of love : herein lies the whole contribution of mysticism. About this twofold love the mystic will never have done enthusing. His description is interminable, because what he wants to describe is ineffable. But what he does state clearly is that divine love is not a thing of God : it is God Himself."[51] Bergson remarked, when speaking at the Edinburgh Philosophical Society, in 1914, that "God is the creator of creators." Regarding creation he says, "Creation ........ is God undertaking to create creators, that He may have, besides Himself, beings worthy of His Love."[52] This denotes that God can have no purpose in creation excepting a mere love for creation.

The Love and Joy are inherent in His being. Creation is nothing other than the outcome of Love to create the lovers of His Being, of Joy to create the sharers of His Joy. God is also described as Joy. "God is there and the Joy is boundless."[53] 'There is an unmixed Joy, lying beyond pleasure and pain which is the final state of the mystic soul.'[54] Creation is a matter of Love and Joy for God. In Love and Joy there is no purpose. If we attribute any inferior motive to these higher purposes, then we shall be subordinating God to this motive. In fact God cannot be subordinated to our purposes.

**The Immanent and the Transcendent God**

According to Bergson, the transcendent cause of the world is God. This conception is similar to Spinoza's conception of *Natura Naturans*. Bergson attributes reality also to the creative force. This force is nothing but God in his immanence. However, both Spinoza and Bergson differ on one point : Spinoza says that objects follow from the nature of the reality according to the necessity of his Being; Bergson, on the other hand, states, that creation follows from the nature of his Being which is Love. This Love is a creation of the lovers of his Being. For Bergson, the immanent creativity also is God. Reality is God. He attributes full reality to the transcendent God. The élan vital which is the immanent reality therefore is not beginningless. It realizes itself in the universe. The transcendent is *eternal* and *complete.* The immanent reality is *'temporal'* and *'on the way of completion.'* Therefore, Becoming is not unreal. It is seeking after reality and when this will be completed, then, there would be no difference between the immanent and the transcendent reality.

**Artistic Creation Through God's Love**

Nature raises up souls that are more detached from life. If the detachment is complete, the soul no longer cleaves to action by any of its perceptions. Now, the soul is that of an artist. Such a soul would perceive all things in their native purity : the forms, colours, sounds of the physical world as well as the subtlest movements of the inner life. But even here, nature has made artists on one side[55] of their senses only. In one direction only has she forgotten to rivet the perception to the need. Since each direction corresponds to what we call a *sense*—through one of his senses, and through that sense alone, is the artist usually wedded to art. Hence, originally, the diversity of arts.[56]

In the varied arts, the creative power of the individual or the essence of divinity is revealed. The essence of divinity which is God's love appears both as a person and creative power. In the creation of a novel thing, the individual becomes joyful and sees the love of God. As Bergson has said earlier, God thus becomes the object of love and He Himself is Love. Just like the artists the mystics who are also endowed with God's Love lead society to realize the noble ideals. 'As a matter of fact, the mystics unanimously bear witness that God need us, just as we need God. Why should He need us unless it be to love us? And it is to this very conclusion that the philosopher who holds to the mystical experience must come. Creation will appear to him as God undertaking to create creators, that he may have, besides himself, beings worthy of his love.'[57]

So far, we have seen that Bergson describes God as Love and Creation and the artist's or individual's creations are the essence of divinity or God's Love.

## 4. A CRITICAL ESTIMATE

The reference to God in Bergson's Philosophy (before Bergson wrote his *The two Sources of Morality and Religion)* is almost absent except his reference to God in *Creative Evolution* as a centre from which worlds shoot out like rockets in a display of fireworks, the centre being qualified in such a way as to leave no room for doubt that he meant by it no Being who could be regarded as a creator or generator of the process of evolution, but that it was synonymous with the process of evolution itself. Another significant feature of *Creative Evolution* is that it is not determined by an end or purpose. It is completely purposeless.

Reality or God in *Creative Evolution* is Change. It is a tendency or an *impersonal push.* But when we come to his *The two Sources of Morality and Religion,* we see Bergson referring to God freely and frequently. He even favours Christianity. What made him to arrive at this conclusion suddenly? What happened to his philosophy of 'Becoming' in *The two Sources?* God in *The two Sources* is certainly not 'Becoming.' He is almost a 'Being.' But this 'Being' is in no way related to the 'Being' of Parmenides because for Parmenides 'Being' is a thing bereft of its attributes. But for Bergson, God is Love and Creation.

When Bergson says that everything in this world changes in *duration,* he makes no room to conceive a Being who can see the past, present and future simultaneously. Duration is something in which the past survives in the present. The future is unforeseeable. In his later work when he accepts God, he must attribute to it the consciousness of simultaneity of the past, present and future. Otherwise He is not God. For Bergson God is not just like an engineer who constructs buildings. Then why does Bergson talk of God? Henry C.

Corrance says regarding this : 'His philosophy, though, concrete, forbids the glazing over and confusing of real distinctions, such as that between duration and eternity. These two ideas cannot be compared from his standpoint, the one being founded on a real inner experience, in which all preceding moments are gathered into the present, and the present is always passing on to the future; the other being a mere abstraction, detached from, inconsistent with life. In eternity there is neither past nor future. In duration the future is yet unborn and the past exists only as it lives in the present. The idea, then, of God as a Being who gathers up all succession, past, present, and future, in one simultaneity of consciousness, amounts to nothing more than the complete and absolute spatialising of duration. No juglery of logic can ever unite such totally and essentially opposed ideas as those of succession and simultaneity.'[58] From the standpoint of Bergson, it is very difficult to contemplate the idea of God.

Ralph Tyler Flewelling, a personalist substituted for Bergson's Duration a person. To his thought the self-referring subject of experience is the only reality of which duration can be affirmed. To the person, past, present and future present themselves as a single experience related to one another. Whether we agree with the above view of Flewelling or not when he talks about the shift of Bergson's thought with regard to the Élan Vital between *Creative Evolution* and *The two Sources*, we have to agree with him. The philosophy of change emphasises the impersonal, indefinite and indetermined nature of Reality (Élan Vital). This is purely metaphysical. *The two Sources of Morality and Religion* identifies the Élan Vital with the world ground. 'It is no longer an impersonal push. It is a creative energy which can love and can desire love, which can create in purposive way'.[59] Though we do not call Bergson a personalist, there is no doubt that by favouring Christian mysticism in *The two Sources*, Bergson makes the readers to come to a conclusion that Bergson is a personalist. Is Christ not a human being according to Biblical accounts? Why does Bergson attribute Love (which is specifically applicable to human beings) to God?

When he comes to dynamic religion, Bergson identifies it with the Christian mystical experience. In the mystical experience, God becomes to the experiencer an élan. Mysticism for many centuries had been explained by assuming the real existence of the Being with whom the mystic believes himself in communication. Further than this, the vital energy launched across matter, whether appearing from within or above consciousness, is one with consciousness and of the same kind. This élan appears in religion, in music, or in art. This is more than intelligence and something more than understanding and nothing but *élan vital*, or creative energy. It is also described as,

> "A creative energy which would love and which desired to draw from itself beings worthy of love, could thus cast forth the worlds of matter to oppose the divine spirit that he might express simply the distinction between that which is created and that which creates."

Bergson does not hesitate to take the extreme personalistic position that man represents the purpose of life on earth—"l' home, qui est la raison d' etre.....". Thus, he has prepared the way for the existence of the soul. The same method is used by Bergson in the case of the philosophic God. Both God and soul should be conceived only in terms of living experience. The physiological explanation of memory is insufficient. The soul must be taken as a unit of experiences and hence the possibility of its survival.

In his youthful days Bergson was severely criticised because of the impersonal character of his élan vital. Bergson in his *Les Deux Sources de la Morale et de la Religion* undermines most of the criticisms and shows himself the exponent of those tenets dear to philosophy—God, freedom, and immortality. In his earlier work he had the doctrine of freedom and in his later work he has the doctrine of God or of the enduring self. So, there is no wonder that the vital impulse of *Creative Evolution* is being identified with Divine Love and Creation in *The two Sources.* Thus the philosophy of *Becoming* is transformed into personalism in which a *Being* is a *must.*

## REFERENCES

1. Bergson : *Creative Evolution*, p. 262.
2. Henry C. Corrance, "*Bergson's Philosophy and the Idea of God*", *The Hibbert Journal*, Vol. 12 (1913-1914), p. 374.
3. Quoted as Bergson saying in A.D. Lindsay's, *Philosophy of Bergson*, p. 19.
4. H.W. Carr : *The Philosophy of Change* (1914), p. 146.
5. *Ibid.*, p. 147.
6. Henri Bergson : *Creative Evolution*, p. 24.
7. Darcy B. Kitchin : *Bergson for Beginners* (1914), p. 199.
8. H.W. Carr : *The Philosophy of Change*, p. 148.
9. Bergson : *Creative Evolution*, p. 60.
10. H.W. Carr : *The Philosophy of Change*, pp. 152-53.
11. *Ibid.*, p. 155.
12. *Ibid.*, p. 156.
13. Bergson : *Mind-Energy* (1920) trans. by H. Wildon Carr, p. 57.
14. *Ibid.*, p. 73.
15. *Ibid.*, p. 55.
16. Dhirendra Mohan Datta : *The Chief Currents of Contemporary Philosophy*, p. 257, (1950).
17. Bergson : *Mind-Energy*, p. 5.
18. Bergson : *Creative Evolution*, pp. 107-110.
19. W.T. Stace : *A Critical History of Greek Philosophy* (1956), pp. 293-94.
20. H.W. Carr : *The Philosophy of Change*, p. 163.
21. *Ibid.*, p. 164.
22. Bhavana Purushottamdas Trivedi : "An Examination of the concept of change, with special reference to the Philosophies of Bergson and Buddhism" (Ph.D. thesis, Poona University, 1973), p. ii.
23. Bhavana Purushottamdas Trivedi : 'An Examination of the concept of change, with special reference to the Philosophies of Bergson and Buddhism' (Ph.D. thesis, Poona University, 1973), pp. 12-13.
24. *The Creative Mind* : Bergson, trans. by M.L. Andison, pp. 227-228.
25. *Creative Evolution*, p. 313.
26. *Ibid.*, p. 174.
27. *Ibid.*, p. 2.

28. *Ibid.*, p. 2.
29. *Ibid.*, p. 3.
30. *Ibid.*, p. 4.
31. *Ibid.*, pp. 4-5.
32. Bergson : *Matter and Memory* (Paris, 1896), Chapters II and III.
33. *Creative Evolution*, p. 5.
34. Bergson : *Creative Evolution*, pp. 5-6.
35. *Ibid.*, p. 6.
36. *Ibid.*, p. 6.
37. *Ibid.*, pp. 320-324.
38. Consult on this Dr. Einstein's own work of which the translation by R.W. Lawson had been published : *Relativity : The Special and General Theory*, Methuen, 1920.
39. La Perception due Changement : Bergson, Lecture 2, p. 24. Deux conferences faites a l'universite d'Oxford, les 26, et 27 Mai, 1911.
40. *Ibid.*, p. 37.
41. H.W. Carr : *The Philosophy of Change*, p. 195.
42. Cited in Annales de Philosophie Chretienne, March, 1912; Quoted in Henri Bergson, by Ruhe and Paul, p. 42.
43. *The two Sources of Morality and Religion*, p. 225.
44. A.C. Bhattacharya : *Sri Aurobindo and Bergson*, p. 174. (Italics not in the original).
45. *The two Sources of Morality and Religion*, p. 207.
46. Frank Thilly : *A History of Philosophy*, p. 108.
47. *Ibid.*, p. 109.
48. *The two Sources of Morality and Religion*, p. 209.
49. *Ibid.*, pp. 208-9.
50. *Ibid.*, p. 216.
51. *Ibid.*, p. 216.
52. *Ibid.*, p. 243.
53. *Ibid.*, p. 219.
54. *Ibid.*, p. 249.
55. According to Bergson artists can perceive nature *directly* through their five senses. For ordinary people there is a veil between their senses and the nature and so the yare not able to see it directly. But even for artists, adds Bergson, the veil is removed to any one of their senses only and hence the diversity of arts.
56. Bergson : Laughter trans. by Cloudesley Brereton and Fred Rothwell, pp. 154-55 (1921).
57. *The two Sources of Morality and Religion*, p. 218.
58. Corrance, Henry C. : '*Bergson's Philosophy and the Idea of God*', The Hibbert Journal, Vol. 12 (1913-1914), pp. 379-80.
59. Ralph Tyler Flewelling, '*Bergson and Personalism*', *The Personalist*, Vol. XIV, 1933, p. 89.

*Chapter IV*

# Intellect and Intuition

## Life and Knowledge

Bergson maintains that theory of knowledge and theory of life are inseparable.[1] To know knowledge by itself is incomplete if we do not have the history of its development. History of knowledge implies the history of life. In other words there is mutuality of knowledge and action. Action involves life. 'The theory of life, then may illuminate the theory of knowledge if it shows us more clearly the history of the mutual interaction of thought and action.'[2] Creative Evolution is largely concerned with this history. We see in the evolution of life from its lowest to highest forms the life continually winning new triumphs over the obstacles of matter. It is also defeated by the very instruments which helped to get its triumphs. When the habits act as obstacles to life they hinder the power of adaptability to new circumstances which is the essence of life.

## Thought and Action

Man's thought is the greatest of the instruments which life has invented. The development of thought has raised him above all other forms of life. But thought itself by its very success, in solving some of the problems of life become set in habits. These habitual tendencies and interests hinder it from solving those problems. In ordinary action the purposes of conscious life are set against the world in which they are to be satisfied. The external reality acts as matter upon which life sets its forms for temporary starting points and ends and so the highest interest of life to apprehend reality is affected by distracting the life. This is possible for an ordinary action which disables thought in the fulfilment of its highest interest.

**Development of Practical Thinking into Science**

The necessities of immediate action are mostly met by the language we use and the action may be enabled for the use and development of thought. But these necessities have already set their mark upon language, so that it is instinct with certain assumptions which are useful in ordinary action, but fatal to its speculative interests. This results in our thoughts being shaped by the influence of practical ends even when we seem to be concerned with purely theoretical inquiries. The ordinary practical thinking thus develops into science which aims at analysis and practical proof. The development of ordinary practical thinking into organised sciences makes the mind free itself from the close subserviency of immediate practical ends. To free itself furhter from the more subtle influences of these ends it is necessary for the mind to rise from science to philosophy.

**Inadequacy of Science**

Science because of its limitations can not give an account of some of the problems of evolution. This was evident from the fact that both biology and psychology failed in their attempts to give adequate explanations of the problems and their solutions. Recognising individualities of their own, biology and mathematics gave different natures of their subject-matter. Bergson points out in *Creative Evolution* the success of science in the inorganic sphere with its failure in the sphere of life. 'The human instinct feels at home among inanimate objects, more especially among solids, where our action finds its fulcrum and our industry its tools.... our intellect triumphs in geometry, wherein is revealed the kinship of logical thought with unorganised matter..... our thought in its logical form is incapable of presenting the true nature of life.'[3] Any number of attempts to distinguish sharply between these spheres of reality break down. A purely quantitative presentation of inorganic matter is impossible, because we can not ignore all qualitative differences. The fact that it is impossible to ignore the quantitative differences is because it makes the conception of motion possible.

**Duration has two kinds of Intelligibility**

Bergson adds that on the other hand duration can contain both quantitative and qualitative differences. Therefore, the contrast of two kinds of intelligibility is found within the sphere of duration itself. Even though mathematical conception of conscious life is contradictory it is impossible to regard life as lying altogether outside the sphere of mathematical inquiry. We need not therefore deal with two separate and distinct spheres.

**Intelligence and Intuition**

Science indeed is more at home in the sphere of the inorganic. It can be applied to life. Intuition is the method of apprehending external phenomenon as it is which is harder to realize. Without such a realisation we can give only an inadequate explanation of them. The difference between intelligence (to use the word which, in *Creative Evolution,* Bergson applies to the strictly scientific method) and intuition is partly a difference of methods accounted for by a difference of sphere; intelligence is more adapted to the inorganic, intuition to life. There is also a difference of purpose between the two. In spite of their differences Bergson does not keep them in water-tight compartments because both of them are not independent of each other. Each uses the other in its functioning.

**Reality—the Combined Development of Science and Philosophy**

Philosophy can not completely ignore the scientific

method, science being a reaction to feeling or the irrational. Intuition must be more rational than science. As there is progress in life, it should combine with scientific method an element which that advance has neglected. 'Reality itself, in the profoundest meaning of the word, is reached by the combined and progressive development of science and philosophy.'[4] The distortion of reality by intelligence by neglecting the individual is elaborated by Bergson in the contrast between instinct and intelligence. In *Creative Evolution* it is part of his exposition of the connection of theory of life with theory of knowledge. These two faculties are specialised forms of consciousness each having something that the other lacks. Intelligence has won its great achievements by its development which is one sided and to become philosophy it has to acquire something more.

**There is no Sharp Division between Instinct and Intelligence**

Bergson when comparing instinct and intelligence says that even though a sharp contrast is made between these two, in all conscious life both these tendencies present themselves, instinct predominating in animals and intelligence in human species. He pictures instinct as it would be if intelligence were entirely absent from it, intelligence as it would be devoid of instinct, while insisting that in reality this sharp division does not exist. If we examine the behaviour of animals we can note their organs functioning in such a way that they are highly developed to meet the special situations as though they anticipated such situations. Whereas if these animals were to meet quite other simple difficulties which were unfamiliar to them their instincts no longer were useful to them. A paralysing wasp behaves towards its victim *as though* it were 'a learned entomologist and a skilful surgeon in one.'[5] Anyhow in an unfamiliar situation the wasp is entirely helpless.

**Nature and Functions of Instinct and Intelligence**

The nature of instinct is a puzzle to us, because we take for granted that a power of dealing intelligently with one situation implies a power of dealing with another situation related to it, provided that the second is not more complicated. As opposed to instinct, the characteristic of intelligence is its adaptability, its power of grasping the general element in a situation, and relating it with past situations. This power is got by losing the perfect mastery over a special situation in which instinct rules.

Modern industry, dominated by scientific inventions and methods, encourages general adaptability and kills craftsmanship. The advantages and defects of machine production as compared to skilled handicraft bring out the point of Bergson's contrast between instinct and intelligence. In his attempt to connect thought and action he connects intelligence with the invention and development of tools. The last stage of the development of intelligence is modern machines. The instruments of animal's action are parts of himself and are organic. The organic instruments have got only limited ranges; but they are perfect and more complex. Man's power is tremendous because of his use of inorganic tools which have got wideness of range. 'The contrast between skilled handicraft and machine production shows us that the contrast which Bergson makes between instinct and intelligence finds its place also within human activity'.[6] The intimate connection between the hand of the craftsman and the matter on which he works makes us feel that the matter can hardly be distinguished from his hand. So, also the relation between the violinists' fingers and his bow, which just because it is something infinitely more subtle that could be expressed in rules, we naturally call sympathy. Since this skill is specialised it has a relatively narrow range. On the other hand the machine works by repetition and it has no individuality.

## Intellect is Conceptual, Symbolic and Definite

The methods of thought and their application to rules to the most varying material make us neglect the individualities between objects and to know only their common relations. This tendency of thought is called by Bergson as intelligence. The doctrines which Bergson is combating count reality as consisting of repetitions of identical parts. They ignore the individuality and movement of reality. Individuality can not be reduced to rules. Science attempts to manifest reality in the way the above doctrines try to do. Intelligence uses words as tools. Its concepts are regarded as fixed and definite. We can use and manipulate them as though they were tools. The application of tools depends on the principle of repetition and the law of causation that the same produces the same. The intellect works with what is given and does not attempt to apprehend the individuality of the real, but to 'reconstitute it with given, and consequently with stable, elements.'[7]

## Logic has the Basis of the Law of Identity

Logic considers the relations between the individualities of things independently. So, it is 'the complete set of rules that must be followed in using symbols.'[8] Its principles go back ultimately to the law of identity. The methods of logic whether by deduction or induction are based upon the same law of identity. 'Intuition implies that qualities can be superimposed on each other like magnitudes.'[9] Such a logic therefore views the world as a thing manufactured. The individual according to the metaphysics of such a logic is considered as a mosaic put together of previously existing elements. This is also construed as a time process as a series of pictures made into one motion resembling the separate snapshots of a cinematograph film.

## Bergson's Criticism of Logical Analysis

Language and logic are criticised by Bergson for it would seem to reduce intelligence to a bare apprehension of identity. Formal logic without the matter of thought has been discarded. Even though Bergson assails the logic of identity and joins hands with the critics of such logic, Bergson's criticism are more far-reaching than those of former critics. Unlike the previous criticism of the logic of identity he not only rejects its wrong conclusions, but also discovers the roots of its errors.

There are also two objections to Bergson's account of intelligence. Bergson connects intelligence with space and measuring and especially with mathematics. So, the logic and metaphysics which he attacks are based upon the mathematical sciences. But we cannot say that mathematics is the outcome of the movement of thought which is based only upon the law of identity because mathematics involves imagination and the insight of genius. In this respect mathematics does not depend upon repetition and also it is not a mere reconstruction of the given.

### Intelligence—the Reversal of Thought Process

Though the machine may be mechanical, its inventions is not so. Invention requires insight of genius. Bergson does not say that concepts themselves are the works of intelligence. In *Time and Free Will* we see that each member as in itself the work of an individual intuition. Bergson says in *Creative Evolution* that geometrical intelligence is something rigid and incapable of evolution. This has been criticised by his critics and to them he answered in the *Revue de Metaphysique et de Morale* (January, 1908) that it is only a misrepresentation. The meaning of his statement is clear in the *Introduction to Metaphysics* where he is concerned with the contrast between intelligence and intuition. 'A more profound history of human thought would show that we owe to it all that is greatest in the exact sciences as well as all that deserves to live in metaphysic. The greatest of the methods of inquiry at the disposal of the human spirit, infinitesimal analysis, came from this reversal of thought...... that method has only been able to attain to its wonderful applications through the invention of definite symbols, and if intuition as we describe it, originated the invention, it was the symbol alone *that made the application possible.* But metaphysic, which *is not concerned with application,* can and must refrain from translating intuition into symbols.'[10]

**Bergson is not against Pure Mathematics**

Bergson does not criticise the principles of mathematics, 'but the *assumptions* underlying the application of mathematics. He is not denying the reality of mathematical universals, but asserting that they are not the only universals. There is imagination and intuition in pure mathematics, there is none in the use of a table of logarithms or tables of compound interest.'[11]

**Plato's Views on Intuition**

The distinction between intuition and its application is maintained not only by Bergson but also by Plato. According to Plato mathematical truth is certain and infallible and can be distinguished from its application to the world of becoming and decay. The first is knowledge and the second is not and cannot be, knowledge. Whenever Plato is talking of knowledge he is thinking of the apprehension of the pure universal. Since the ordering of the particulars of the world of sense is the use made of the apprehension it partakes of the infinite, the application of mathematical truth cannot be knowledge. 'Plato is one with Bergson in insisting that true knowledge must dispense with symbols. For both, knowledge is immediate apprehension, an act of the spirit.'[12] But Bergson disagrees with Plato in that he says that the latter considers universal as the type of all universal and hence had to deny the reality of change and time.

**Kant**

For Kant the problem is completely different. He is not

concerned with the validity of the mathematical truth : his problem is how the mathematical truth is applicable to the world we perceive with our senses and how the truths which our understanding apprehends can be held *a priori* to be valid of the world which is given to perception. But modern thinkers are more particular about the usefulness of the truth, its coherency, its systematic nature and its results when applied.

A modern thinker like Bertrand Russell distinguishes between what is and what exists which revives Platonic distinction of the world of knowledge and the world of opinion. Even though Bergson shares the modern views of the biological sciences, he follows Plato when he says that instead of studying the facts of life indirectly by the application to them of mathematical principles, they can be apprehended with insight of philosophy.

## Bosanquet's Criticism of Bergson's Views on Induction and Deduction

Bergson criticises both induction and deduction for their dependence on mathematics. Professor Bosanquet, in a paper read before the Aristotelian Society criticised Bergson's views on induction and deduction and added that induction was not merely a principle of identity but a real universal. Induction implies a process of active thought and insight which could not be reduced to rule.

## Bergson's Criticism of Causal Theory

In empirical science and in causal theory Bergson finds no satisfaction. The view that like produces like is untenable according to Bergson because it ignores the process of change which could not be reduced to identity. In an event or a change all the preceding changes have to be taken into account. If we isolate a particular cause-effect phenomenon we are ignoring the preceding changes and therefore it is misleading. Bergson's above criticism of causal theory also adds that there can be no particular individuality for an event and reality is a system in which there are no qualitative differences.

Leaving the nature of the causal relation, if we observe what is implicit in its application to other cases we have the following analysis of causal theory : "To see that A cause B requires insight and apprehension of individual characteristics. When we say 'This is like A, and therefore its effect will be like B', we are applying a result of that insight, and we are concerned with Ā only in so far as its resembles A. That implies that Ā repeats A, for its difference with A must for our purposes be ignored."[13] In a process of real change repetition is impossible. In applying our apprehension of causal relation we effect an artificial isolation. Moreover in science we are tracing causal relations which tries only to find individual differences and thereby isolating the system of reality into various states of cause. The changes which are initially simple become complex and the older elements have to be viewed in a new perspective. In his attempt to ignore repetition and quantitative analysis Bergson is concerned with intellect as opposed to intuition. Since the causal relations have to be apprehended by the methods other than those which guide their application, apprehension of causal relations by intellect is impossible. However, intuition and intelligence are not isolated, though they are contrasted tendencies of thought. Both intelligence and intuition involve each other in the process of thought.

**Limitations of Scientific Knowledge**

Intellect or the application of intuition also makes possible prediction along with its implication of repetition. Unlike philosophy, science is concerned with application because from its practical interests it is concerned to predict. The real distinction between intuition and intelligence lies, in their criterion of truth. Verification of intuition is not possible because the test of mathematical truth lies only in its apprehension. For science the criterion is to say, 'If such and such conditions are arranged, such and such results will follow' which implies that the experiment can be repeated. Science, because of its ignoring the individual differences is inadequate especially when it deals with life-sciences. When we are dealing with individuals we note that there is a common structure for them. But they are not identical. It requires therefore insight to see the common character of the results of the experiment. The difference between intuition and intelligence disappears when a method other than mathematical is applied to construe the individual differences of cases. When such a method is applied science is becoming more like philosophy. If we insist that the ideal of scientific method must be mathematical, in the study of life we are confined to those characteristics which repeat themselves and here we have to ignore the individual differences of cases. The results apply only to the mass and not to any one individual. This is evident in the application of statistical methods to the sciences of life. They are concerned with mass results and averages and most of the calculations are approximate. The calculations are just like chances in gambling, the results of which hold for, 'the long run' of the game. It cannot be applied to any individual throw. In any single throw we are concerned only with the conditions and environment and ignore the causes which determine the result of any single throw. What is to happen, 'in the long run' may never take place because the determining causes of individual cases are ignored. A biometrician or a sociologist has the averages of the mass results which ignore the activity of the individuals. This may result in altering the conditions with which the statistical methods are concerned. Legislation modifies the external conditions of life. It relies therefore upon statistical methods. By relying upon these for apprehension of historical change we ignore the part played by individuality in history.

Sciences by ignoring individuality gain their exactness and this is confined only to spatial relations where individuality can be ignored. In the sphere of life the prediction of science is not certain. The prediction of science to be certain, has to adopt the method of philosophy. By having an insight into the development of life we can have the immediacy of insight into mathematical truth. The difficulty lies in the nature of the reality we have to apprehend.

If the mathematical relations are self-contained, then the mathematical insight is certain. All relevant data can be had in one synthesis. A process whose limits go beyond our perception both in space and time has to be synthesised. But we can never attain this because our synthesis is always imperfect. Intuition should not therefore dispense with science and rather it should supplement it. 'Concepts', says Bergson, "are indispensable to it, for all other sciences work with concepts, and metaphysic cannot do without the other sciences."[14]

**Intuition—the Intellectual Sympathy**

How intuition is different from science? It attempts to apprehend reality as it is in itself. Science is particular about the purposes of action. Because of this science is not disinterested unlike art. Intuition like art is disinterested or rather interested only in its object. Intuition implies sympathy because it cares to know things in their own nature.

Sympathy is understood by Bergson in a further sense that it enables to assume the nature of other things. It also feels with them. "It is impossible to have an intuition of reality, that is an intellectual sympathy with its innermost nature, unless its confidence has been won by a long comradeship with its external manifestations".[15] The passage preceding the above will make Bergson's point clearer : 'This faculty is in no way mysterious. Every one of us has had opportunities to exercise it in some degree. Any one, for example, who has been engaged in literary production, knows perfectly well that after long study has been given to the subject, when all documents have been collected and all sketches made, one thing more is necessary—an effort, often painful, to set oneself in the heart of the subject and get from it an impulse as profound as possible, when there is nothing more to be done than to follow it. This impulse, once received, sets the spirit on a path where it finds again all the information it had collected and a thousand other details. The impulse develops itself, analyses itself in expressions, whose enumeration might be infinite, the further you go on, the more is revealed; never can you say everything that is to be said; and yet if you turn back to apprehend the impulse you feel behind you, it is hidden from you. For it was nothing but a direction of movement, and although capable of infinite development, it is simplicity itself. Metaphysical intuition seems to be of the same kind. Here the counterpart of the sketches and documents of literary production is the totality of the observations and experiences collected by the positive sciences'.[16]

**History is both Science and Art**

All empirical inquiry implies a process which cannot be reduced to rules. The process in itself is a creative act. There are two suggestions showing that the process, if vaguely described, does not imply vague and nebulous thinking. The first is the well-known passage in Plato's Seventh Epistle, where we can observe his metaphysic, "It cannot be put into words as can other inquiries, but after long intercourse with the thing itself and after it has been lived with, suddenly, as when the fire leaps up and the light kindles, it is found in the soul and feeds itself there."[17]

What is emphasised here is that though our language and instruments of our inquiry are inadequate we should not give up those instruments. Instead to overcome this inadequacy we should make use of perceptions and definitions and the apprehension of the real will suddenly flame forth. The second suggestion is the example of history. History implies scientific method and careful analysis of particular facts. But it is more than a science because it required insight for a historian to synthesise all the facts for which there are no rules. It is more than a science in the sense that its facts are not the mere outcome of laws, or the inevitable unrolling of a plan known from the beginning. If it is mere outcome of the laws, individuality of its subjects are ignored and facts are distorted. 'History never repeats itself.' History therefore is both science and art. It follows science in the wideness and comprehension of its scope and mastery of detail; it is like art in that it is the work of genuis'.[18]

**Analysis and Synthesis are Indispensable**

Verification implies repetition and therefore neither history nor philosophy admit of verification in the ordinary sense of the word. The insight of a historian makes us know the details of history and its facts. Philosophic intuition likewise must be faithful to the facts of science. Bergson in his philosophic method separates tendencies which in reality are never separate : duration and extensity, quality and quantity, time and space, instinct and intelligence. These do not lie side by side in reality. But to understand reality analysis is necessary. Only by an act of synthesis we can see the whole and the act is an intuition. Both analysis and synthesis are indispensable. Only 'by rubbing the two together' can the flame of intuition burst forth.

**Intellect and Intuition—the two Ways of Knowing Reality**

The reality revealed by the above method of philosophy can be apprehended in the process which requires both intuition and analysis. Both exact sciences as well as the intuitive sciences are the two aspects of reality. Bergson identifies movement with the intuitive science and permanence in that movement with exact science. According to him there are real movements. Since reality of movement or change implies time and as time implies individuality, the real movements are individual. Discontinuity of our needs and purposes make us reduce movement to a series of states or points. If we are to rise above such practical implications of thought we must recognise that our duration does not stand over against a timeless world, but is one among other durations. We should understand other movements if we could apprehend them as we can apprehend the process of our own consciousness. Therefore, there is not one duration, but many durations. But even though it seems they are discontinuous they are not entirely separate. As is evident from the examination of the biological methods it is hard to make absolute divisions between the various forms of life as between the different members of a species. All life is one in the sense there is some kind of common impulsion. Individuality admits of degrees and there are different 'rhythms of duration'. So, individual systems are more or less closed, and discontinuous with the rest of reality.

**Two kinds of Movements in Bergson's Metaphysics**

The fact that there are degrees in individuality make us to admit that the distinction between intelligence and intuition is one of degree. In the process of duration we have two aspects : the act of thinking and thoughts. Separating the thoughts from the act of thinking we have only a series of associated ideas. In so far as conscious life is such a series of associated ideas—this is, in so far as we are not actually thinking—It is not free. It can be scientifically studied. These ideas and memories are the basis of thinking. "Each of our acts of thought becomes in its turn a memory, and the basis for further acts. The creative movement of life implies the same two aspects. Its creations have a basis of habit, and in their turn become habits. Its movement is a process of synthesis to new forms, but it is accompanied and made possible by another movement towards fixity and repetition and sameness. The artists' fingers may be painting a picture which, because it is a creation, could not have been predicted, and was not contained in the past; but all the time they are dispensing energy which has been stored up in a special form in his muscles, and in his brain cells. This downward movement can be calculated just because it is a movement from mobility to fixity. It can be regarded as necessary, because there is no more of it in the end than in the beginning. Its limit is a homogeneous medium where qualitiative differences have disappeared."[19]

Exact sciences through universal mathematic eliminates qualitative differences in a movement. Thus, it conceives movement and change apart from us. From this we cannot predict or reduce to mechanical terms its growth or its production of novelty. If science constructs a methaphysic from its ideal it can discriminate in a movement a series of points through which it passes; but it is not possible from a series of points to construct a movement.

Bergson and Kant sail in the same boat when they assert the validity of mathematics. But for Kant "what was outside of the sphere of mathematical application was outside of the sphere of knowledge"[20] because he was concerned wholly with the mathematical sciences. Bergson's limitation of the sphere of mathematical inquiry makes room for another method of inquiry which attempts to solve those problems created by mathematical sciences.

## REFERENCES

1. *Creative Evolution*, p. XIII.
2. Lindsay, A.D., *The Philosophy of Bergson*, p. 213 (1911).
3. *Creative Evolution*, pp. X, XI.
4. *Ibid.*, p. 210.
5. *Ibid.*, p. 153.
6. Lindsay, A.D., *The Phisophy of Bergson*, p. 220.
7. *Creative Evolution*, p. 173.
8. *Ibid.*, p. 169.
9. *Ibid.*, p. 228.
10. Bergson : Introduction to Metaphysics, p. 43. Underlined passage by A.D. Lindsay, *The Philosophy of Bergson*, p. 225.
11. Lindsay, A.D. : *The Philosophy of Bergson*, p. 226.
12. *Ibid.*, p. 227.

13. *Ibid.*, p. 230.
14. *Introduction to Metaphysics*, G.T.P. 13.
15. *Ibid.*, G.T.P. 57.
16. *Ibid.*, p. 56.
17. Plato : *Epistles*, vii, 341, 344.
18. Lindsay, A.D., *The Philosophy of Bergson*, p. 240.
19. *Ibid.*, p. 246.
20. *Ibid.*, p. 247.

*Chapter V*

# Intellect : In the two Sources of Morality and Religion

We have seen the intellect in contrast to intuition and matter in *Creative Evolution*. In his *The two Sources of Morality and Religion* Bergson applies the intellect to ethical and religious spheres. It is seen that the application here of the intellect acts as counterpart to the dualism of closed and open rationalism.

## 1. APPLICATION OF INTELLECT TO MORALITY

Bergson shows in *The two Sources of Morality and Religion* (1932) the affinity between habit and everyday morality. In this regard he is influenced by his predecessors *Maine de Biran and Ravaisson.* Throughout his work, Bergson indentifies habit with reason (or intellect for our convenience) which can be narrowed down to 'closed' or 'constituted' reason, because this is the only kind of reason which Bergson recognises. There is no need for Bergson to distinguish closed rationalism from open rationalism. Though Bergson did not attempt to explore such distinction suggested, much post-war existentialist philosophy (in which ethical considerations are latent) has done no more than elaborate the dualism put forward in *The two Sources of Morality and Religion.*

### Obligation, Social Law and Morality

Bergson begins by analysing the idea of law in *The two Sources* and the way in which the double use of the 'law' is confused in most people's minds. The double use of the word implies on the one hand, the natural regularity of phenomena and on the other hand, the means of maintaining order in society. The scientist normally maintains the distinction; but at the same time he remembers that "a law promulgated by society is backed by force, and that this threat, it is hoped, will induce the waver to conform, although of course he *can* disobey. A human law is an expression of the collective will, which seeks to prevail over the aberrations of individual wills. A law of nature, however, is not the outcome of anybody's will; it is merely an account of the order and manner in which things happen. But just as people tend to think of such natural laws as dictated by a higher power, so inversely do they come to think of the decrees of society as having the unquestionable force of the natural order".[1] Bergson adds in this regard that "the law borrows from the command its prerogative of compulsion; the command receives from the law its inevitability."[2] So, the commonest characteristic of any single obligation is this appearance of inevitability. Consequently people hardly question their duty. Not only do they not question their duty but also they question not their thought; hence obedience to duty is 'a form of non-exertion, passive acquiescence.'[3] Most of the moral philosophers do not agree with the above contention of Bergson. They hold that obedience to duty involves tension and struggle with oneself. Morality becomes interesting only when such self-conscious effort is present. Since this self-conscious effort arises from inner strife, it is not surprising that the idea of obligation is associated with that of self-discipline and self-compulsion. But basically according to Bergson the sense of obligation is 'a tranquil state, akin to inclination'.[4] This kind of response to obligation is very similar to the semi-automatic performance of any non-moral act. This also resembles to the 'quotidienneté' (quotidien = the everyday) of more recent writers which is brought out by Bergson when he remarks that only rarely do acts involve a moral struggle. He also adds that 'Consciousness is this hesitation itself, for an action which is started automatically passes almost unperceived.'[5] Since the French word 'conscience' means both 'awareness' and moral awareness it cannot be rendered here adequately. Our effort makes its impact on consciousness. Where there is no effort, our mental life proceeds in a kind of 'lethargic passivity.'

**The Closed Morality**

Social laws, duties and rules which we have seen so far are in accordance with the species of social requirements. They should change their nature if they have to inspire people. "We do not feel proud or gratified to have paid our income tax or parked our car clear of the Fire Station exit."[6] These imperatives are hypothetical in nature and are aimed at social preservation. The laws which the society imposes on its members concern very much with the furtherance of its interests. If the members adhere to these aims they may become good citizens of the society and it does not suffice to make them *good men,* at least by the highest standards. "Between the nation and humanity lies the distance separating the finite and the indefinite, between the closed and the open."[7] Bergson shares the view of Andre Lalande, that attachment to family, party or nation will not liberate us from the demands of egoism. The closed morality is also characterised by its partiality, limited loyalty and even perhaps a sublimated self-love which is different in kind from the universal love of humanity. The universal love of humanity does not aim at power-seeking. It is the true negation of all power-seeking. Bergson clearly distinguishes the two :

"Whereas the former is all the more unalloyed and perfect precisely in proportion as it is the more readily reduced to impersonal formulae, the second, in order to be fully itself, must be incarnate in a privileged person who becomes an example. The generality of the one consists in the universal acceptance of a law, that of the other in a common imitation of a model."[8]

### The Closed Morality arises out of Pressure from Society

We are here seeing the opposition between universalist and existentialist ethics : the one belongs to the world of legislation, the other to that of inspiration. Closed morality is social and open morality is what Bergson calls 'human.'[9] The word human must be understood "in the sense in which Sartre uses it in the expression 'human reality' : a morality or a reality in which the person is the origin and measure of the world which he bodies forth by his own participation."[10] The closed morality is restrictive and tends to dehumanise. The open morality is expansive and moves constantly away from the objectified values embodied in maxims and universal, impersonal ordinances. "Whereas natural obligation is a pressure or a propulsive force, complete and perfect morality has the effect of an appeal."[11]

### From the Closed to the Open

The move from the closed to the open is by way of what existentialists would call a leap, or conversion. There is no natural progression from one to the other. A limited loyalty, however intense, is of a different nature. There is absolute discontinuity between the two worlds : "It is not by a process of expansion of the self that we can pass from the first state to the second."[12] The force corresponding to social pressure here apart from instinct and habit, is feeling. Only feeling can exert a direct action on the will. Strong feeling or passion has got something in common with obligation; "it exerts a compelling force on its victim, who is not necessarily under the illusion, at the outset, that he is pursuing his own pleasure. His future may be fraught with tragedy and he may be aware of this, but it makes no difference. The tragedy of passing in conflict with obligation resembles the situation of the man faced with a truly 'costing' moral choice. So, creative activity in art, science and civilization, says Bergson, is owed most often to new feelings, felt and communicated through the force of great personality or ability, or both."[13]

## The Open Morality

In his conception of the open morality, Bergson stands at the end of one tradition, and at the beginning of another related one. Open morality is owing to a model who is imitated and who initiates a new way of feeling. In this regard Bergson looks back to the Christology. Divinity is seen incarnating through history in exceptional individuals. Bergson follows for his Christology the traditions of Strauss, and Renan. According to Renan, Jesus brought into existence a new manner of feeling. This is the novelty of Christianity. The message of incarnationists is that humanity puts the best of itself into its gods and heroes. But personalism and existentialism have betrayed the above philosophy. It is therefore necessary to look beyond the cult of the moral hero for the nature of authenticity.

Bergson points out that emotion can be either owed to an anterior idea or representation, its status being then that of an induced or secondary experience, or it can relate to an idea which it brings about, thus becoming a cause and no longer an effect. There is no significant distinction between artistic and moral creation according to Bergson. For most people it requires something outside them as stimulus to cause emotions. This is the prime requirement of the creative artist. "Such intellectual power as is needed to provide moral revolutions is infused with feeling, and the amalgam is 'the intelligence which invents', and which is to be distinguished from and preferred to 'that intelligence which understands, discusses, accepts or rejects—which in a word limits itself to criticism,' and is what (literally in a word) Bergson always understands by reason."[14]

## Raymond Polin on the Closed—the Open Morality

Similar to Bergson's distinction between the closed and open ethic we have M. Raymond Polin's between norms and values in *La Creation des valeurs*. Bergson's view that the social order exerts a pressure on the individual is reasonably obvious. But many people find it difficult to understand how creative morality can exert the attraction of an emotion which we desire to share. And this is because we cannot usually rediscover the original emotion in ourselves. But we can find "formulae which are the residue of this emotion."[15] Very close to this Polin would say : norms which are the residue of this value. Closed value according to Bergson, is something solidified and immanent in material reality. Open or true value is transcendent and derealized in the fire which burns in creative activity and its communication, and there alone. He reduces the distinction between the closed and the open to that "between repose and movement."[16]

## Open Morality is Dynamic

This accounts for the case with which closed morality, compared with the other, can be described and formulated. No doubt, intelligence and language deal with things, but are less at home in representing transitions or progressions or change which is dynamic. 'The morality of the Gospels is essentially that of the open soul'. We have Jesus on the Mount preaching the Sermon in which He contrasts the universalised social ethic (Ye have heard that it was said .....) with his own message (I say unto you.......). He adds that the conventional morality is not discarded but comes to be seen as comprising so many particular instances of a dynamic teaching. Bergson says that we have significantly, a comparable relationship between pagan and Christian morality. This is similar to the relationship between the mathematics of the ancient world and the differential calculus.

## Socrates is a Mystic—Bergson

Socrates in Bergson's views is also a mystic whose "teaching, so perfectly rational, hinges on something that seems to transcend pure reason."[17] He is described as an open soul who set the feet of philosophy firmly on the path of closed rationalism and morality. So, the personality of Socrates contradicts his teaching. His teaching is the apotheosis of the activity of reason and the aim of his dialogues is the production of concepts amenable to definition. Furthermore, he applies this logical approach to ethics, and makes virtue a science : "he identifies the practice of good with our knowledge of it,"[18] and aims to absorb moral life into the rational function of thought. This supreme apostle of reason has a mission enjoined by the oracle of Delphi; he is poor, and yet he must remain so; he must speak a language of the people and he is for them; since his words must be a living force his teaching is an oral one. He is guided by his 'daemon' to the end. He can enjoy the good things of life. He can also withstand cold and hunger. In short he is a mystic.

**Repetition and Creation**

'Repetition' and 'creation' are the words used by Bergson to represent two moralities. He says that somewhere between these two lie detachment and contemplation, which have attracted some of the greatest minds. Among them are Plato and Aristotle. This is the meeting ground for thinkers of many persuasions. But this detachment is no more than a 'half-virtue' because the modern attitude is that a complete virtue is inseparable from action.

**Justice—the Manifestation of the Dual Morality**

Justice is pre-eminently the field in which the dual morality manifests itself. The justice in law-courts is closed justice because it is quantitatively established and represented as holding the scales for the precise apportionment of what the law lays down. Here legislation is interpreted and applied. Equity is equality. This originates in exchange and barter and involves the exact assessment of the value of the objects exchanged. Justice relating to objects is extended to cover intercourse between persons, where the idea of obligation attaches itself to that of equity in the exchange of actions. Therefore, injury naturally demands an equal reciprocity. This kind of justice is sophisticated; but it is "faithful to its mercantile origins."[19] What bridge is there from this justice to that expressing the inviolability of rights and the impossibility of measuring the human person in terms of any values whatsoever? Justice evolves gradually from a primitive state of injustice. However, at some point we see that there is discontinuty. A leap has occurred. This was not foreseen earlier. What is the reason for this leap? It is due to some exceptional individuals who are the best in humanity. They come forward and persuade society to change its attitude. The laws and regulations of a closed morality is thus modified by "a series of appeals made to the conscience of each of us by persons who represent the best there is in humanity."[20]

## Bergson's Self-contradiction

What is the best in humanity? There seems to be some question—begging because according to his philosophy of evolution the future is unforeseeable. In the above context Bergson has to conclude that 'there is a pre-existing entity which corresponds in some way to the ultimate goal of open morality,' into which "reality is....... eating its way........ incorporating into itself, bit by bit, the totality of eternal justice."[21] Here Bergson is practising what he has condemned. The absolute ideal to which future mankind is committed is characterised by Bergson as the universal brotherhood. This is a contradiction to what Bergson had said earlier : (i.e.) the future is unpredictable.

## Bergson's Position Defended

Bergson's position is defended by saying that his conception of open morality is not progressive. It is only reminding the man of an eternal excellence to which he must try to conform. It is further stated in defence of this ideal that "there was no question here of clear-cut wisdom, reducible from beginning to end, into maxims. There was rather a pointing of the way........."[22] Maxims could be dispensed with. So, no heed had to be taken of particular circumstances, historical, geographical or sociological. Inspiration is at work in the open morality. Relevant means will be found once inspiration is at work. Restatements of a general moral appeal can be varied. This will result in producing historical results bearing no relation to each other. Gospels are the basis for some of the most tightly closed systems of morality. A number of repressive regimes were the product of individualistic urges. These were revolutionary in tradition. The basic general precept of civilized life is, "Do to other as you would wish them to do to you." But this is liable to be stultified in practice because people have to be treated in different ways. In the army one man takes the hectoring of his superiors as a personal insult. Another man takes it as a comical affectation. Therefore, the difference between the closed and open morality is the difference between straight-forward orders (*e.g.* Thou shalt not kill) and dispositional recommendations. The latter cover a great variety of actions and attitudes. Its relevance must be found by the moral agent. The business of the moral agent is to judge and act upon.

### Bergson, the Fore-runner of the Closed—the Open Rationalism

We have discussed both closed and open morality. It is obvious that the question whether it is true to say that the application of intellect includes open morality also will arise. Because in the foregoing discussions we have seen that Bergson holds the view that the word 'repetition' can be identified with closed morality and the word 'creation' can be identified to open morality. In fact Bergson's metaphysics also states that the nature of intellect is static and repetitive in nature. What is dynamic and flowing is intuition. So, there is every reason not to include open morality in the fold of intellect and its application to moral and religious spheres.

As we have already seen in the beginning of this chapter recent French rationalistic philosophy has developed a distinction between closed and open rationalism. This was done because of the influence of the closed and open morality conceived by Bergson. Hence rationalism includes both 'closed' and 'open' rationalism traceable to Bergson's 'closed' and 'open' morality.

## 2. APPLICATION OF INTELLECT TO RELIGION

### What is Religion?

We have seen how Bergson applied his concept of intellect to moral sphere. Now, we will see how he applies intellect to religious sphere. Before going deep into Bergson's views of religion let us see how other thinkers have talked about religion. William James, the American philosopher-psychologist who influenced Bergson very much in writing *The two Sources of Morality and Religion* through his *The Varieties of Religious Experiences* says, "Religion therefore as I now ask you arbitrarily to take it, shall mean for us *the feelings, acts, and experiences of individual men in their solitude, so far as they apprehend themselves to in realtion to whatever they may consider the divine.* Since the relation may be either moral, physical, or ritual, it is evident that out of religion in the sense in which we take it, theologies, philosophies, and ecclesiastical organisations may secondarily grow."[23] Apart from this definition of William James there are others who consider the religious sentiments which are referred to in so many books as if they were a single sort of mental activity. The psychologies and philosophies of religion have attempted to specify just what entity it is. One man traces the origin to the feeling of dependence; another derives religion from fear; others connect it with sexual life and some others identify it with the feeling of the infinite and so on. The different ways of conceiving religion arouses doubt in us. Whether it is one specific thing or 'religious sentiment' is a collective name for the many sentiments which religious objects may arouse in alternation. It contains nothing whatever of a psychologically specific nature. "As concrete states of mind, made up of a feeling *plus* a specific sort of object, religious emotions of course are psychic entities distinguishable from other concrete emotions; but there is no ground for assuming a simple abstract 'religious emotion' to exist as a distinct elementary mental affection by itself, present in every religious experience without exception. As there thus seems to be no one elementary religious emotion, but only a common storehouse of emotions upon which religious objects may draw, so there might conceivably also prove to be no one specific and essential kind of religious object, and no one specific and essential kind of religious act."[24] Emile Durkheim defines religion thus : "A religion is a unified system of beliefs and practices relative to sacred things, that is to say, things set apart and forbidden—beliefs and practices which unite into one single moral community called a Church, all those who adhere to them"[25] Clifford Geertz defines : ........ "a religion is : 1. a system of symbols which acts to; 2. establish powerful, pervasive, and long-lasting moods and motivations in men by; 3. formulating conceptions of a general order of existence; 4. clothing those conceptions with such an aura of factuality that and 5. the moods and motivations seem uniquely realistic."[26] This definition is highly abstract. Anthony Wallace writes : ....... "religion is a set of rituals, rationalised by myth, which mobilises supernatural powers for the purpose of achieving or preventing transformations of state in man and nature."[27] By 'transformations of state', Wallace refers to day-by-day changes in life conditions, important and unimportant, large-scale and small-scale. He sees little value in distinguishing between religion and magic. "Religion is the attempt to relativize the individual's desires, as well as his fears, by subordinating them to a conception of absolute good more in harmony with the shared and often mutually contradictory needs and desires of human groups."[28] Edgar Sheffield

Brightman says, "The great practical result of religion in human history has been to convince man that his natural desires ought to be controlled in the light of the ideals shared by a just and supreme judge. Thus religion is a program of individual and social self-control."[29] In W. Schmidt's opinion, "Religion may be defined both subjectively and objectively. Subjectively, it is the knowledge and consciousness of dependence upon one or more transcendental, personal powers, to which man stands in a reciprocal relation. Objectively it is the sum of the outward actions in which it is expressed and made manifest, as prayer, sacrifice, sacraments, liturgy, ascetic practices, ethical prescriptions and so on."[30]

Radhakamal Mukherjee is of the opinion that "Religion arises out of man's normal relations to his environment. The distinctive feature of religious experience is that man creates an ideal world which resolves the conflicts or stresses of his normal mental life and evolution. He thus develops a certain permanent attitude towards the physical and the social environment. Such a permanent attitude comes of a more or less complete fusion of his impulses, and this makes his adjustment to nature and to society easier, more stable and effective."[31]

## Bergson's Views on Religion

According to Bergson morality, whether it is closed or open is concerned with the influence of our actions. We do this directly or indirectly. In each case we make some sort of appeal to human initiative. Moral influence is turned inwards towards the human. When our initiatives are turned outwards from the human we have, *objectively*, scientifc activity. When the initiatives are turned inwards subjectively we have magic or mysticism. The turning of human initiative both subjectively and objectively are the two poles of religion. Bergson divides religion into two : static religion and dynamic religion. These two divisions are based on his metaphysics.

**Static Religion**

Static religion consists of beliefs and rites. It is the body of doctrine to which people subscribe. They have different forms of worship and faith. They adhere to their faith. If we look for the origin of static religion we have primitive psychology than philosophy. The characteristic of primitive religion is myth-making. The social function of this is to provide a barrier against the disruptive activity of intelligence. Man is the only animal whose actions are uncertain. He hesitates and lays plans in the hope of success and the fear of failure. He is alone to realize that he is subject to illness. He is alone to know that he must die. The rest of nature goes on its expanding course in absolute tranquillity. Of all the creatures that live in society, man alone can swerve from the social line. He give sway to selfish preoccupations when the common good is at stake. In all other societies the interests of the individual are subordinate to the general interest. This two-fold shortcoming in man is due to his intelligence. This is the price paid for intelligence. To exert his faculty of thought man has to imagine an uncertain future. This rouses his fears and his hopes. Nature has made man a social being. As long as he is a social being he has to think only about himself and his own needs. He finds it more profitable if he ignores other members of the society. So, he cannot think about what nature demands of him. There is a break of the normal and natural order of things. Yet it was nature who ordained intelligence. It placed it at the end of one of the two great lines of evolution. This is a counterpart to the highest form of instinct, which is the terminal point of the animals. Nature is fully aware of the disturbance caused by intelligence to the condition of order. The same nature which provided intelligence to man tends to restore order by giving some other thing which belongs to intelligence itself. Thus to re-establish the social order automatically, nature has given myth-making function of intelligence to man. Myth-making is not pure intelligence; but its object is to counteract the dangers caused by intelligence. Its role is to elaborate that religion which we have discussed so far. It is therefore called as natural religion. So, the static religion is defined by Bergson thus : "It is a defensive reaction of nature against what might be depressing for the individual,, and dissolvent for society, in the exercise of intelligence."[32]

**Bergson's Illustration of Static Religion**

To illustrate the above statement of Bergson, an example given by him deserves mention here. He shows how the myth-making function of intellect comes for man's rescue when the actual intelligence fails : "A lady was on the upper floor of an hotel. As she wanted to go downstairs, she walked out on to the landing. The gate provided for the lift happened to be open. As the gate was so contrived as to be open only if the lift were stopped at that floor, she naturally thought the lift was there and rushed forward to take it. All of a sudden she felt herself flung backwards; the man entrusted with the working of the lift had just appeared and was pushing her back on to the landing. At this point she emerged from her fit of abstraction. She was amazed to see that neither man nor lift were there. The mechanism being out of order, it was possible for the gate to be open at her floor, though the lift was still down below. She had been about to fling herself into the gaping void; a miraculous hallucination had saved her life. Need we say that the miracle is easily explained. The lady had reasoned correctly on a real fact, for that gate was really open and therefore the lift should have been at that floor. The mere sight of the empty shaft would have been enough to show her, her mistake; but it would have been too late, the action consequent upon the correct reasoning being already under way. It was then that the instinctive or somnambulistic self, which underlies the reasoning personality, came into action. It had seen the danger, it had to act at once. Instantly it had thrown her body backwards, at the same time inducing in a flash the fictitious, hallucinatory perception the best fitted to evoke and explain the apparently unjustified movement."[33]

**Static Religion is a Defensive Reaction of Nature against Intelligence**

For the bee-hive and the ant-hill nature has provided instinct. Here instinct is co-extensive with life. Social instinct in insects is nothing more than the spirit of subordination and co-ordination animating the cells and tissues and organs of all living bodies. In insects, the development of instinct is towards expansion of intelligence. Man, though has got intelligence, does not mean that he has no instinct. Instinct in him is eclipsed. So, also intelligence in vertebrate and invertebrate animals is eclipsed. For the progress of the society stability must be there among the members. If man were a slave of instinct, like ant and the bee, he would remain intent on the purely external object to be attained. Automatically and somnambulistically he would have worked for the species. Since he is endowed with intelligence he will turn to himself and think only of leading a pleasant life. But nature is on the watch. Just like, before the open gate a guardian appeared to save the lady, protective deities of the city will be there to forbid, threaten, and punish. So, *looked at from this first point of view, religion is then a defensive reaction of nature against the dissolvent power of intelligence.*

We cannot separate intelligence from conscious action. In primitive societies what is done in the interests of all is done unquestioningly. This is done even by force of habit. This is desirable also because if we question law it would weaken it. In societies such as ours there are customs and laws. The laws are often stabilised customs. A custom becomes a law only when it is of particular, recognisable and definable value; then it stands out from among the others. We have the distinction between what is custom and what is legal or moral obligation. The distinction can also be termed as between the essential and the accidental. In less advanced societies we have only customs. Some of these customs are justified by a real need. Most of them are justified due to mere accident. All customary things are here obligatory. The customs are accepted by all. They have not yet been condensed into laws. Everything habitual to the members of the group, everything that society expects from individuals, is bound to take on a religious character. This is true because the observance of custom attaches man to other men and thus detaches him from himself. So, in rudimentary societies it is noted that the question of the relation between morality and religion is greatly simplified. Primitive religion can only be called non-moral. It is indifferent to morality. This can be seen when we take religion as it was in the beginning and compare it with morality such as it became later on. "Originally the whole of morality is custom; and as religion forbids any departure from custom, morality is coextensive with religion."[34] So, the objection that religious prohibitions have not always dealt with things that strike us to-day as immoral or anti-social is baseless. Primitive religion is a precaution against the danger man runs. The danger is due to his selfish-thinking. Therefore, it is a defensive reaction of nature against intelligence.

**Static Religion Stems from Myth-making**

The above view of Bergson is held by many other thinkers also. One of the main characteristics of static or primitive religion is myth-making. About this P. Thomas says, "Just as strata of earth give an indication to the life of the earth and even of the progress of life through prehistoric times, myths are thought-fossils which teach us in allegories and symbols the story of cultures and civilizations that preceded ours, and the attempts of primitive man to solve various human problems."[35]

Bronislaw Malinouwski describes myth thus : "Myth as it exists in a savage community, that is, in its living primitive form, is not merely a story told but a reality lived. It is not the nature of fiction, such as we read to-day in a novel, but it is a living reality believed to have happened in primeval times, and continuing ever since to influence the world and human destinies......... These stories live not by idle interest, not as fictitious or even as true narratives; but are to the natives a statement of a primeval, greater, and more relevant reality, by which the present life, fates, and activities of mankind are determined, the knowledge of which supplies man with the motive for ritual and moral actions, as well as with indications as to how to perform them."[36] It is also defined by Larousse thus : "Myth is both an inspiration and protection for any one who lives like this; it is a model for present action and a justification of it. But the words that we are forced to use to describe this fundamental experience, life according to myth (which has its being in the obscure zone preceding the emergence itself), are dangerous and deceptive. Myth is not chosen after intellectual deliberation because it can be adapted to action; it is an instinctive choice, accepted with all one's being, and it is compounded more of faith than reasoning. Myth is one of the elements of consciousness; in the collective consciousness it exists as a reality, which finds an echo in the individual consciousness as language sometimes does."[37]

Renan expressed concern for the abandoning of religious belief. This, in his opinion would leave the human destiny, being controlled by 'untrammelled intelligence!' If the analytical and critical activity of intelligence were allowed free play, the will to act would be weakened. For primitive man, as Bergson and Renan see him, reason is the way towards anti-social temptation. The social significance of myth-making is seen in the fact that myth always bears traces of its origin. In its origin, "it will never clearly distinguish between the physical order and the social and the moral order, between intentional orderliness due to the obedience of all to a law, and the orderliness manifested in the course of nature...... Does not the word 'order' signify both system and command."[38]

## Civilized Societies are not Exceptions to Myth-making

Bergson shows that even in civilized man there appears the rudimentary creations of myth-making function virtually endangered. With its humanised figures, the myth is already a sophisticated product. In our society the taboos and reassurances are so numerous. So, it is very difficult to build them into coherent accounts. Consequently, we have fragmentary myth-making functions. These produce adhoc bridges between reality as it is and as we would have it. *e.g.* The belief in immortality, the animal tendency to invoke individual spirits, friendly or hostile etc. The former is required in a society which consists merely of individuals and which withstands the ravages of time. The latter inhabit objects and places of everyday life. These can be rationalised as continuous with those other parts of experience which are under human control. These fill up the unmanageable gaps in experience, presenting an element of personality. Man thus inhabits a world which is 'physiognomic'. He has a kind of animated responsiveness, real or imagined, to our requirements. Phenomenology has its own intentional world. It is among other things a reminder of the role of this physiognomic realm in civilized man.

## Myth-making is nature's turning intelligence against itself

The fabrication of intentional entities according to Bergson is the work of intelligence. This erects a barrier against the depressing incursion into human life of inanimate, meaningless and random reality (the concept of which is itself the work of intelligence). From this it is clear that a sympathetic study of 'primitive' mentality throws light on modern misgivings about the 'dehumanising' potentiality of science. This it is feared will reduce everything to mechanism, even human feelings and motives. Bergson, then distinguishes science and magic. He does not find any origin of science in magic. They have different functions and different provinces. Science deals with natural causality. Both primitive and civilized man use it. Magic deals with supernatural causality. This is analogous to human will and has to be induced. In Bergson's view the myth-making function is a case of nature's turning intelligence against itself. But we will not qualify superstition from any identification with intelligence in any form. Anyhow Bergson states that any non-intuitive mental activity is intellectual. The synthesis of these two orders of Causality (natural and supernatural or scientific and magical) is unscientific. It is well articulated picture of reality. However, this is primitive. Closed religion has this in common with closed morality. But Bergson contrasts this reality with that known through mystical intuition.

We had already seen the first function of religion (*i.e.*) social preservation. We must remember that the sphere of life is essentially that of instinct. Along a certain line of evolution instinct has to some extent made room for intelligence. This will lead to a disturbance of life. In such circumstances, nature has no other resource than to set up intelligence against intelligence. The intellectual representation which thus restores the balance to nature's advantage is of a *religious* order. So, as its first function religion preserves society by myth-making faculty of man's intellect.

**Static Religion is the Defensive Reaction against the Fear of Death**

Now, let us come to the second function of religion. We know that animals do not know that they must die. Some of them make the distinction between the living and the dead. The sight of a dead creature and of a living one does not produce in them the same reactions. This does not imply that they have a general idea of death. An animal will 'sham dead' to escape from an enemy. It is we who define its attitude thus. So far as it is concerned, it does not stir because it feels that by moving it would attract attention and invite attack. Cases of animal suicide have also been reported. There is a vast difference between doing what must result in death and knowing that the result is going to be death. Suppose that an animal has the notion of death. He certainly does not realize that he must die a natural death if he does not die a violent one. It is not useful to an animal that he must die. It is better for it not to know that he must die. But man knows that he will die. All other living creatures are simply carried along by impetus. Since with man reflection appears, his observations include the field which may not be useful for his immediate requirements. With his intelligence man compares his observation with another, deduces and generalises the results from his observations. He sees that every living thing about him ends by dying. He is convinced that he will also one day die. Nature, in endowing him with intelligence, must inevitably lead him to this conclusion. The thought of death, therefore causes for man's anxiety and depression. The impetus of life turns all other living creatures away from the image of death. Only in man the thought of death slows down the movement of life. This depressing thought would be more depressing, if man were not ignorant of the date of his death. The certainty of death therefore runs counter to nature's intention. Nature, then looks as if it is going to stumble over the obstacle which she has placed on her own path. But she recovers herself at once. She relieves man from his depression by giving him a new hope. *She assures man that there is life after death.* This idea that there is life after death neutralises man's idea of death. This simply expresses the equilibrium of nature. So, 'looked at from this second standpoint, religion is a defensive reaction of nature against the representation, by intelligence, of the inevitability of death.'[39]

So far, we have seen two essential functions of religion. For these two functions, the primary tendencies and general forms were the same. Now, the third function of static religion has the same method. As usual we postulate as certain instinctive activity. We, then, call intelligence into play. We try to discover whether it leads to a dangerous disturbance; if it does, the balance will probably be restored through representations evoked by instinct. Such representations are religious ideas. These ideas were aimed at 1. social preservation, (*i.e.*) assurances for the members of the society against their depression caused by the selfishness of certain members of the society and 2. assurances against the inevitability of death. Let us now see the third function of static religion.

**Static Religion is the Assurance against the Unforeseeable**

In the case of an animal nothing intervenes between its aim and act. If it sees its prey, it pounces upon it. "If it is a matter of lying in wait, its waiting is a forestalling of the act and will form, with the accomplishment of it, an undivided whole."[40] In the case of the bee building the hive, the ultimate objective is remote. It is an objective of which the animal is unaware. It only sees the immediate object. The leap it takes is exactly co-extensive with the act it has to accomplish. But it is the very essence of intelligence to co-ordinate means with a remote end. Intelligence, here undertakes what it does not feel absolutely sure of carrying out. "Between what it does and the result it wants to attain there is more often than not, both in space and in time, an interval which leaves ample room for accident."[41] Circumstances must lend their aid if the beginning has to be finished successfully. It is fully conscious of this margin of the unexpected. The savage, when the shooting his arrow, does not know if it will strike the object at which he aimed. In the case of the animal with its prey, there is continuity between gesture and result. But in intelligence there is no such continuity. A gap appears, exposed to accident, attracting the unexpected. In theory intelligence is constituted to act mechanically on matter. It thus postulates a universal mechanism. It conceives virtually a complete science which would make it possible to foresee, at the very instant when the action is launched. It tries to foretell everything that is likely to come up against before reaching its goal. The ideal here is never fulfilled because human intelligence is confined itself to very limited action on a material about which it knows very little. But the vital impulse ignores the accidental and the unforeseen. In a word it avoids the indeterminate which lies along its path and advances by leaps and bounds, seeing only the end in view, devouring the space between.

Yet it is necessary that intelligence should have cognizance of this anticipation. Accordingly there arises a representation of favourable powers. It over-rides or occupies the places of the natural causes and continues into actions ordained by them. It acts according to our wishes on natural lines. So, we have two kinds of mechanisms working here : one set by us in the beginning and another in the realization of the desired effect, that is the end. Between the two there is a super-mechanical guarantee of success. When we imagine that friendly powers are responsible for our success, then it is inevitable that our intelligence will imagine that unfriendly powers are responsible for our failure. But according to Bergson the hindering force developed only later. In fact the consequence of the development of the helping force is the development of the hindering force. Especially in primitive societies the latter grew because in stagnant societies beliefs multiply indefinitely. Such beliefs multiply by means of analogies without any regard for their origin. But the vital impulse is optimistic. It gives hopes and assurance against the unforeseeable. So, the third function of static religion can be defined thus : *"They are defensive reactions of nature against the representation, by the intelligence, of a depressing margin of the unexpected between the initiative taken and the effect desired."*[42]

**Myth-making Function**

Bergson discusses this function from evolutionary point of view. The vital impulse as had been conceived by him in *Creative Evolution aims* at the progress of the species to new destinies. Dividing itself into three main directions (Plant, Animal and Man) the vital impetus evolves uncesasingly. The challenges of life are met by the animals by their instincts. But in man there is intelligence which is not as quick to action as instinct in animal. Intelligence works out on the materials supplied by the sense-organs. So, it takes time for it. It is not helpful to man to act immediately. The vital impetus has given a remedy for this to man by giving him the faculty of myth-making which serves his immediate purposes. Myth-making, even though, is part of the function of intelligence, actually aims at counteracting the dangers caused by the intelligence. Intelligence acts selfishly which may cause for the disorganisation of society. This is against the intention of the vital impetus. So, it engages intelligene against intelligence. This counterpoise cannot be by instinct itself. However according to Bergson, there is some residue of instinct surviving on the fringe of intelligence in man. This is called by Bergson as *virtual instinct*. This cannot act on man directly. Since intelligence works on represntations, the virtual instinct calls up 'imaginary' ones which hold their own against the representation of reality. Thus, the virtual instinct succeeds through the agency of intelligence itself in counteracting the work of intelligence. Thus, the vital impetus maintains order and progress by myth-making in human societies.

When we say that myth-making function is nothing but imaginary ideas we have yet to distinguish poetry and fantasy of all kinds from religion. In this regard Bergson says, "very likely, therefore, poetry and fantasy of all kinds appeared as extras, benefiting from the fact that the mind knew how to make myths, but religion is what accounts for the myth-making function : faculty standing to religion in the relationship of effect and not of cause."[43] Susanne K. Langer distinguishes fairy-tale from myth, thus : "For the fairy tale is irresponsible; it is frankly imaginary, and its purpose is to gratify wishes, 'as a dream both flatter.' Its heroes and heoines, though of delightfully high station, wealth, beauty, etc., are simply individuals; 'a certain prince', 'a lovely princess'. The end of the story is always satisfying, though by no means always moral; the hero's heroism may be slyness or luck quite as readily as integrity or valour. The theme is generally the triumph of an unfortunate one—an enchanted maiden, a youngest son, a poor Cinderella, an alleged fool—over his or her superiors, whether there be kings, bad fairies, strong animals (*e.g.* Red Riding Hoods Wolf), stepmothers, or elder brothers. In short, the fairytale is a form of 'wishful thinking'....... Myth, on the other hand, whether literally believed or not, is taken with religious seriousness, either as historic fact or as a 'mystic' truth. Its typical theme is tragic, not utopian; and its personages tend to fuse into stable personalities of supernatural character."[44]

Bergson is criticised for his stand that myth-making is an activity of intelligence. Bergson says "that an essentially intelligent being is naturally superstitious, and that intelligent creatures are the only superstitious beings."[45] But Colin Smith holds that the evolutionary drive is diametrically opposed to the work of reason.[46]

## Magic

Myth-making function differs from magic. Gods, deities, spirits, etc., are connected with mythology. But these forces are mechanical and are not complying with our wishes. They are not bending to our will. So magic deals with the spirits which are complying with our wishes. It is innate in man. It is the outward projection of a desire which fills the heart. (*E.g.*). A man in his wrath performs the act of looking his fingers about his (absent) enemy's throat. Here the *static replaces the dynamic* because a living enemy is contemplated in a static imaginary form. Magic comes under yet other laws: "it is possible to influence a being or a thing by acting on something it has touched", "the part is valid for the whole etc." *E.g.* "In time of drought, the sorcerer is asked to produce the rains. If he were actually to put his whole soul into the task, he would, by an effort of imagination, raise himself upto the cloud, he would believe that he felt himself cleaving it asunder, and scattering it in rain-drops. But he will find it simpler to suppose he has nearly come back to earth again, and then to pour out a little water; this minute fraction of the event will produce it in its entirely........"[47]

In Bergon's opinion, then, magic can be resovled itself into two elements : "the desire to act on a thing, even on that which is out of reach, and the idea that things are charged, or can be charged, with what we should call humarı fluid."[48] The first is concerned with the comparison between magic and religion.

**Magic and Science**

Science measures, calculates and analyses with a view to anticipation and action. All progress in science consists in a wider knowledge and a richer utilization of the universal mechanism. First, it supposes; then it verifies. Finally, it comes to a conclusion that the universe is governed by mathematical laws. Even though science acts on matter, matter present in the whole universe is not under its control. For example, the faculty of sight is meant only to reveal to us objects on which we can act. But, though we see stars we have no control over them. So, nature has given us along with the faculty of understanding the matter we have to deal with, *a virtual knowledge of the rest. But she has not provided us virtual power to utilize it.* Magic then steps in. It acts as an immediate effect of the vital impulse. In primitive man magic invades the realm of science. Magic conceals science in non-civilized man to such an extent as to make us believe in a primitive mentality devoid of all real science. This is so because it costs no effort for him. Its inventions are pure fantasy. But according to Bergson, science and magic are both natural. They have always co-existed. Our science is more extensive than that of our remote ancestors. But the civilized man is less given to magic than the non-civilized man. At bottom both the civilized and non-civilized are remaining the same. In spite of the modern scientific advancements, the civilized man still has the inclination towards magic. If his attention to science is relaxed for one instant, magic will at once come rushing back into his civilized society.

**Magic and Religion**

In a sense magic is part of religion (of course lower type of religion). In common with religion, magic represents a precaution of nature to meet certain dangers encountered by the intelligent being. However, they differ in many respects. In religion we see men praying god. Religion thus conceived undoubtedly is opposed to magic. The latter is essentially selfish. The former demands disinterestedness. Magic compels nature to comply with man's wishes. Religion implores the favour of the god. Above all, magic works in an environment which is semi-physical and semi-moral. The magician is not dealing with a person. On the contrary religion draws its greatest efficacy from the personality of the god. "Magic and religion, then go their separate ways, having started from a common origin, and there can be no question of deriving religion from magic : they are contemporaneous."[49] However some magic lingers in religion, and some religion in magic. The magician works through the medium of spirit. This spirit is individualised. It does not possess the complete personality nor the eminent dignity of gods. Whereas god has personality, dignity, command and prayer.

**Belief in Spirits**

The belief in spirits is primitive. From belief arose adoration, animism and religion. If we trace the origin of the belief in spirits we can note that "man attributed purpose to thing and events, as if nature had eyes everywhere which she focused on man."[50] This is an original tendency in man. That we can all verify this when a sudden shock arouses the primitive man dormant within us all. We feel in these cases the sensation of an *efficient presence.* Whether well or ill disposed, a certain intention of his environment follows him everywhere. If that intention is good he will rely on it; if it is harmful he will try to avert its effects. In any case he has been taken into account. The idea of such intentions of nature increases when he perceives himself, and when he will think of himself as a speck in the immensity of the universe. Thus, if the effort to live did not at once project into his intelligence he would feel lost. He considers that there is some intention in nature turning against him. Here we can see man's effort to live being intellectualised. His own intelligence acts as a barrier in his life by speculating things and events which are funfavourable. On the other hand we see the animal having no such speculations. It does not believe itself to be the centre of the world because it has no conception of the world as such. It has not the slightest inclination to speculate. It only sees and takes note of what can satisfy its needs. It behaves as though everything in nature were combined solely with a view to its well-being and in the interests of its species.

The idea of *efficient presence* then, gave rise to spirits already individualised on the one hand and the idea of an impersonal essence on the other. The idea that there are intentions inherent in things brings us to the representation of spirits. For instance they are dwelling in springs, rivers and fountains. They are vague entities. Each spirit is bound to the spot where it manifests itself. But this spirit is different from divinity. The latter will bear a name; it will have its own particular shape and personality. It presents itself at various places; but it is indivisible. It will only apportion itself between various places. Later on, when religion developed, the spirits became minor deities. But "it took a long time, in Greece, for the spirit of a spring to become a graceful nymph, and the spirit of the wood a hamadryad."[51]

It is also believed that the souls of the dead naturally join with the spirits. Though they are detached from their bodies, they have not yet renounced their personality. By mingling with the spirits they colour them and pave the way for them to become persons. Thus, the spirits advance towards a complete personality. Belief in spirits underlies all religions (Greek, Roman, Hindu, Chinese and Japanese). Even today we can see in India, China and Japan the *ancestor-worship* constituting an important part of life. The human mind passes through the belief in spirits before attaining to the adoration of the gods.

**Deference paid to Animals**

Between the cult of spirits and the adoration of gods there is another thing to be mentioned : the respect paid to animals. As we know already man is depending for his actions on his intelligence and reflection. His weapons and tools invented by his intelligence are not unfailing. But an animal which depends on its instinct acts instantaneously. Its actions are unfailing. Even though it has no power of speech, its silence is contemplated by us, as though it had something better to do than to converse with us. All these things made man to pay deference to animal. It must be noted that it is for some specific quality that the animal is adored. "In ancient Egypt the bull represented strength in battle; the lioness destruction; the vulture, so careful of her young, motherhood."[52] Man's inclination towards actions than beings naturally made him to turn his attention on animals. After having gained control of actions, he wanted to get hold of qualities. These qualities seemed to be present, unalloyed, in animals, whose activities are simple. Their actions are consistent and are set in one direction. So, the adoration of animals was not the primitive phase of religion; but after emerging from it, he had the choice between the cult of spirits and that of animals.

**Totemism**

Animal-worship which we have dealt in the last paragraph differs from totemism; it is concerned with the difference paid to an individual animal. But totemism is the difference paid by man to an animal species as a whole. If we want to recognise a man we do so by distinguishing him from other men; but if we want to recognise an animal we should identify the species to which it belongs. In the first case we see the individual characteristics, whereas in the latter we ignore them. An animal stands essentially as a quality and as a species. The first explains the cults of animals; the second discusses totemism. "Let us take the commonest case, that of animal, a rat or a kangaroo, for example, which serves as a 'totem', that is to say a patron, for a whole clan. The most striking thing is that the members of the clan assert they are one with it; they *are* rats, they *are* kangaroos."[53] If we closely observe the intention of primitive man for his division of the tribes existing then, into so many totems, We would get a more systematic and scientific explanation. The mind of the primitive man has to be analysed if we want to explain totemism. If we say that the primitive man does not identify himself with his totem, we can not come to a conclusion that he takes it as an emblem. The truth lies somewhere half-way between these two extreme explanations. Let us interpret it by our principles : Each totem represents each clan and so each clan constitutes a species. Here the individual characteristics of the animal do not catch our attention. The animal is perceived as a species. Even in a same tribe if two clans are there, they belong to two different totems. They indicate that the two clans are of *different blood*.

The clans into which the tribe is divided are often exogamous : (*i.e.*) marriages are contracted between members of different clans, but not with one clan. This was a general law. In fact totemism itself implies exogamy. "It is easy to understand that it is in the interests of nature to prevent the members of a tribe from habitually intermarrying, the final result in a closed society such as this being unions between near relations; the race would very soon degenerate."[54] The vital impetus is cautious. It has provided instinct to species to solve many problems of life. So instinctively by their habits the tribes split up into different clans within which marriages were forbidden. "This instinct, as a matter of fact, will attain its object by at once causing a feeling of relationship between members of the same clan, and between clan and clan a feeling of being as foreign as possible to each other, for its *modus operandi*, which we can see working in our societies as well, is to diminish the sexual attraction between men and women who live together and who know they are related."[55] If the members of two different clans wanted to express the fact that they are not of the same blood, they would get into the habit of saying that they are not of the same speicies. Corresponding to the biological necessity we search for a need in the living creature. If this need does not create a real and active instinct, an imaginative representation determines the way in which we should proceed. This is latent or virtual instinct present in us. We see such kind of instinct being active at the basis of totemism.

**Belief in Gods**

Belief in spirits has always remained the basis of popular religion. We have seen how myth-making faculty which elaborated it, developed into mythology. There is a gradual transition from spirits to gods. But the differences between them are striking. The god is a person. He has his qualities, defects, and character. He bears a name. He stands in definite relationship to other gods. He fulfils important functions, and above all, he is alone in fulfilling them. On the contrary, there are thousands of different spirits scattered far and wide over the country. They all do the same work; they are described by a common name. This name may, in certain cases, not even possess a singular form. Belief in many gods (polytheism) in fact is considered as the mark of civilisation.

But the progress towards polytheism is not rhythmical. We have also the Egyptian tradition of treating the sovereign as a god. The Emperor receives divine honours during his life time and becomes a god after his death. The senate in Rome deified Julius Caesar. All the Emperors after him namely Augustus, Claudius, Vespasian, Titus and Nerva rose to the rank of gods. Anyhow there is a great distance, for example, between the divinity of a Roman Emperor and that of a Pharaoh. The latter is closely related to the divinity of the chief in primitive societies; it is perhaps connected with the idea of a special fluid, or a magic power, supposed to reside in the sovereign, whereas the divinity conferred on Caesar was a case of mere toadyism, being utilized later by Augustus as an *instrumentum regin*."[56] We learn from the above that in ancient days gods could be born, die and be transformed at the whim of man or by circumstances.

**Mythological Fantasy**

The gods cannot be classified into categories under certain laws. This is because men's fancy and fortuitious circumstances are varied. At the most we can bring out a few main trends of mythological fantasy. Even here no single trend was followed regularly. Our ancestors attributed functions to gods. So, the gods served useful purposes. Evidences for this are seen in Greek, Roman, Indian, Chinese, Babylonian cosmologies. (*E.g.*) "For the sowing there was Saturn; for the flowering of fruit trees, Flora; for the ripening of fruit, Pomona etc. ........In the first rank of the divinities of India figure Indra and Agni. To Indra man owed the rain and the storms beneficent for the soil; to Agni, fire, and the protection of the domestic hearth."[57] The above gods were connected with things. There are also gods who function as guardians of particular groups or communities. There were also wars between rival deities.

**Myth-making and Literature**

We have seen already that myth-making function is

different from imagination. Any representation which is neither perception nor memory is called imagination. Such representations depict neither a present object nor a past thing. To some extent even though myth-making is also similar to imagination, it considers a very clearly defined faculty of the mind : (*i.e.*) creating personalities whose stories we relate to ourselves. Originally myth-making is meant for the preservation of individuals and socialites. The fundamental demand has called into being the myth-making faculty. In the same way the faculty creating novels, dramas and other literary works is being driven by the same force which acts as *'efficient presence'* in myth-making. That is why the dramatist is able to make the theatre audience shed tears. We pass quite easily from the novel of today to more or less ancient tales, to legends to folklore, and from folklore to mythology. Though mythology is not the same thing as novel it was developed in the same way.

**On the Existence of Gods**

As far as religion is concerned the adherence of each individual is reinforced by the adherence of all. (*e.g.*) In the theatre, dramatists' suggestions are readily accepted by the spectators. In this case we have a society just the size of the hall. It endures only just as long as the play lasts.

But the individual belief of god had been supported, confirmed by a whole people. It rests both on the past and on the present. The god is sung by poets and he dwells in temples. He is portrayed by art. Though science does not establish the validity of the existence of the God the universal assent of the people gives guarantee of this truth. Since individual and society condition each other religion is both social and individual in essence. The individual and society thus condition each other, circlewise. This circle was intended by nature. But it was broken by him the day he became able to get back into the creative impetus. This impels human nature forward instead of letting it revolve on one spot. From that day there dates an essentially individual religion. This became afterwards social.

The spirits of ancient people were the direct product of their myth-making faculty. This was natural development. But the gods are different from these spirits. Mythology sprang from a need. This is an amplification of primitive activity. It extends beyond the need in all directions. The interval it leaves between this need and itself is filled with human fancy. This human fancy affects the assent accorded to mythology. This is the same faculty which intervenes and invents. Each time when it invents, the invention is taken separately. It is accepted with the reservation that another would have been possible. "The pantheon exists, independent of man, but on man depends the placing of god in it, and the bestowal of existence on that deity." Such an attitude of man is surprising us. The part comes into being through us; but the whole has its own existence independent of us. In just the same way it could be said that each distinct God is contingent and the gods as a whole or rather the Godhead in general, is necessary. If we logically analyse further we will come to know that there had never been absolute pluralism other than the belief in spirits. Polytheism along with its mythology implies a latent monotheism. Here the multiple deities exist only secondarily. They represent the divine. Bergson holds the view that the absurdities are part of religion. "The movements of a swimmer would appear just as silly and ridiculour to anyone forgetting that the water is there, that this water sustains the swimmer, and that the man's movements, the resistance of the liquid, the current of the river, must be taken all together as an individed whole."[58] So, also if we do not understand the background and the action accompanied by religion, then religion will seem to the rational mind as absurdity. There is no religion without rites and ceremonies. The religious representation is an occasion for these religious acts. If gods exist they must have their worship; but since there is worship, then there must be gods. This solidarity of god with the homage paid him makes of religious truth a thing apart from speculative truth. This has no common measure with speculative truth, and depends, upto a certain point, on man. The rites and ceremonies aim at this solidarity.

**Sacrifice and Prayer**

In dynamic religion verbal expression is immaterial to prayer. Prayer is an elevation of the soul that can dispense with speech. In its lowest form it is not unlike the incantations of magic; it aims at capturing the goodwill of the spirits. But in polytheism, we see prayer occupying a place halfway between these two extremities. Polytheism more generally imposes on prayer a stereotyped form. It is not only the significance of the phrasing, but also the sequence of the words, together with all the accompanying gestures. This imparts to it its efficacy. "What constitutes the reality of a perception, what distincguishes it from a figment of the imagination, is, above all, the whole group of incipient movements which it communicates to the body, and which complete this perception by the automatic beginnings of an action."[59] Such kinds of movements may develop due to some other cause : "but their actuality will flow back just the same towards the representation that produced them, and will practically convert it into a thing."[60]

Sacrifice is an offering made with a view to buying the favour of the god. It is also offered to turn aside the wrath of god. Though no rational mind would permit the horror of sacrificing human beings to god, there is something else in sacrifice : "To begin with, it is generally agreed that sacrifice originated in a repast of which the god and his worshippers were supposed to partake in common. Next, above all, there was a special virtue in blood. As the principle of life, it gave the god strength, and enabled him the better to help man, and perhaps also (but this was a barely conscious idea) it ensured to him a more substantial existence. It was like prayer, a link between man and the deity."[61]

Thus, polytheism with its mythology exalted the invisible powers with which man is surrounded. It puts man in ever closer contact with them. Religious feeling in antiquity was made up of many elements, varying from people to people. To some of the people of India and Persia a philosophy has been superadded with religion. But religion and philosophy always remain distinct. The first will remain essentially action, the second, above all, thought. Philosophy only comes into existence to satisfy more cultivated minds. Religion lives on, among the people, in the way we have described. Religion has got a purpose. The intention of nature is the emergence of religion. We have seen what is meant by the intention of nature. We have also discussed the function that nature has assigned to religion. Magic, animal or spirit worship, worship of gods, mythology, superstitions of all kinds, will seem very complex if we analyse them separately. But, if we take them all together they make up a whole which is extremely simple.

## 3. A CRITICAL ESTIMATE

Bergson sees a constant struggle between matter and consciousness in evolution. Consciousness flows against matter. At every stage, there is a confrontation between matter and consciousness. Matter divides for precision. But thought is continuous. In fact matter and consciousness are the two aspects of the same life force. There is progress only through confrontation. So even though it seems that matter resists consciousness, it is only to complement consciousness. Consciousness, each time utilizes the resistance offered by matter as a fresh opportunity for further advancement. This basic metaphysics of Bergson is threading through all his works. When this is applied in epistemology, we have the Bergsonian opposites of 'intellect' and 'intuition'. In religious and moral spheres his metaphysics shapes into the form of static and dynamic religion and closed and open morality. We have seen the functions of intellect in the previous chapters. We must also note that the resistance offered by the opposing force to the Élan Vital can be construed in three stages : as obstacle, as instrument and as stimulus. "It is an 'Obstacle' because matter is what brings division and precision, and spoils continuity of self. Pure mind or pure thought, despite all its purity, cannot stand alone. Alone, it is powerless. It should be expressed. It is matter again that makes expression possible; and so it is an 'instrument.' Without matter again there will not be any effort. By providing resistance it acts as 'stimulus' for the creative realization of the Élan Vital."[62]

Though we agree that Bergson has not drifted away from his metaphysics in *The two Sources of Morality and Religion* we find it difficult to digest the fact that he agrees with the dogmatic truths of primitive religion and morality. The Élan Vital which is biological in *Creative Evolution* takes a definite shape in *The two Sources of Morality and Religion.* Here it is *applied* directly to social and religious spheres. But in both *Creative Evolution* and *The two Sources* the Élan Vital is evolutionary in nature. In the first, it is biological evolution and in the second, it is ethical and religious evolution. In the former, intellect is the instrument by which matter is evolved, intuition the faculty which can know the Reality as it is. In the latter, intellect is the instrument by which habitual morality is evolved, intuition the faculty giving the higher ethic (in the case of religion the intellect is the instrument by which the traditional religion or static religion is evolved and dynamic religion through mysticism aims at the union of the soul with God or Élan Vital).

Religion degrades the spirit. It animates it into a mere object of pious contemplation. Religion is characteristically concerned with eternity. The religion (static) by magic, totems, myths, superstitions and rituals materialises the spirit. This is in comparison with the Élan Vital being checked by matter. The obstacle makes way for further progress of the life force. The static religion is the stepping stone for the adoption of dynamic religion. P. Lenon in a simple language says about the closed morality and static religion : 'Closed morality........ is an affair of more or less definite (closed) and definable relations rather than of persons : of impersonal duties, that is, duties incumbent upon any person qua standing in certain relations or having a certain status, each individual being related to another not as personality to personality or in virtue of their common humanity (or divinity) but as father to son, husband to wife, ruled to ruler, fellow-citizen to fellow-citizen, colleague to colleague, etc., whereas under the open morality the father, for example, may become son to his son and the wife husband to her husband. It is embodied in more or less definite and definable rules, customs, conventions, condes, institutions. It is, in short, the morality of 'my station and its duties.'[63]

In the above quotation what we have to specifically mention is that the relationship in closed morality is more materialised and in open morality it is spiritualised. The similar relation is seen in Bergson's *Creative Evolution* when he distinguishes intuition from intelligence. The husband establishing his relationship with his wife as wife is the ideal which is harder to realize. So, also the ideal of intuition is harder to realize in our apprehension of external phenomena. But without such a realisation we can only give an inadequate explanation of them. According to Bergons intelligence is more adapted to the inorganic, intuition to life. This is what is implied in Lenon's expression of Bergson's conceptions of closed and open morality—religion in his *The two Sources*. By having so many relationships (*i.e.*) father-son, husband-wife, etc., our intellect forms segments of innumerable units which in Bergson's view have to be avoided. The kind of relation which he emphasises is—the universal relation. There must be only one relation which must be universal. This is what we understand from Lenon's passage that a father must establish a relationship of a son with his son.

By his treatment of the open and the closed, especially in morality we see the Bergsonian efforts to integrate this with his previous philosophy. But what does he mean by assigning two separate sources, one for the closed and the other for the open? The closed is natural. It belongs to primitive man. We can find in ourselves the primitive man if we shed all that we have acquired by education and tradition. The inherited alters our original nature. The open comes from God (or from the Élan Vital). But ultimately there is no dualism. The two sources are only apparent. The closed by cutting off a freshet, from the river of life makes it stagnant and thus different from the original water. But the stagnant water (the specific nature) does not spring from the enclosing banks. It does not also spring from another source than the river. But individual's conduct or belief is different. He derives either from one source (the stagnant pool) or from the other (the river or the river's source, God). Hence, there is no ultimate dualism or two ultimate sources. Bergson explains away the whole of primitive, natural or closed religion by reference to the instinct of fabulation instead of saying that it is partly atleast due to primitive man's instinct for God arrested and perverted by fabulation. The closed has no independent source of its own. It is simply an arrest of the open and would not have existed but for the latter.

In *The two Sources of Morality and Religion* we have many self-contradicting concepts of Bergson. Among them the most important two are the idea of intelligence and Élan Vital. The life force appears to be a kind of evolutionary principle. But yet it aims at the triumph of spirit over matter. This is *involutionary* in nature. It is also unpredictable and random. 'Nature' produces man whose intelligence overshoots nature's intention. Nature, therefore, contrives that man shall, by a further exercise of 'intelligence' in the shape of the myth-making function, be reconciled to that purpose. At a more evolved stage of humanity, mysticism, related to but different 'in essence' from the myth-making function is introduced by Bergson. This is again contrary to nature's intention.

The fact that Bergson's concept of intellect is applied in his *The two Sources of Morality and Religion* and that the morality and religion conceived by intelligence is inadequate is evident from the views of H.B. Parkes. Parkes interprets Bergson's philosophy that man should identify himself with the original vital flux to transcend the static morality and religion. By doing so we have a morality which is supra-rational and not infra-rational. Commenting on Bergson's philosophy of morality and religion Parkes says, "Bergson himself, when he applies his philosophy to the problems of morality, arrives at a somewhat similar doctrine, although he does not formulate it so bluntly. Let us go beyond the ethic of the tribe, he exhorts us—an ethic which is formulated in intellectual terms in a code of laws, and which, though created by nature to meet its own purposes, is now an encumbrance upon the progress of humanity. And let us make unnecessary those religious beliefs which came into existence in order to counterbalance the dissolvent and dispiriting influences of the intelligence. If we identify ourselves with the vital flux itself, if we recover contact with the original fountain-head of the energies of mankind, we shall need neither the guidance of a morality nor the consolations of religion. Such a doctrine would seem to point to a morality of power, beyond conven-tional good and evil, since if the vital flux is to be identified with any one impulse it must surely be that of power. Bergson, however, remembering perhaps his identification of instinct with the sympathetic knowledge given by intuition, insists that the vital flow is love."[64]

## REFERENCES

1. Colin Smith : *Contemporary French Philosophy* (London : Methuen and Co. Ltd., 1964), p. 144.
2. Bergson : *The two Sources of Morality and Religion*, trans. by R. Ashley Audra and Cludelsey Brereton, Macmillan, 1935, p. 4.
3. *Ibid.*, p. 10.
4. *Ibid.*, p. 11.

5. *Ibid.*, p. 10. *Cf. supra*, pp. 103-4.
6. Colin Smith : *Contemporary French Philosophy*, p. 145.
7. *The Two Sources*, p. 21.
8. *Ibid.*, p. 23.
9. *Ibid.*, p. 23.
10. Colin Smith : *Contemporary French Philosophy*, p. 145.
11. *The two Sources*, pp. 23-24.
12. *Ibid.*, p. 27.
13. Colin Smith : *Contemporary French Philosophy*, p. 146.
14. *Ibid.*, p. 147.
15. *The two Sources*, p. 37.
16. Colin Smith : *Contemporary French Philosophy*, p. 148.
17. *The two Sources of Morality and Religion*, p. 48.
18. *Ibid.*, p. 47.
19. *Ibid.*, p. 56.
20. *Ibid.*, p. 68.
21. *Ibid.*, p. 63.
22. *Ibid.*, p. 62.
23. William James : *The Varieties of Religious Experience*, Collier Books, New York (1961), p. 42.
24. *Ibid.*, p. 40.
25. Emile Durkheim, *The Elementary Forms of the Religious Life*, tr. Joseph Ward Swain, London : George Allen and Unwin Ltd., New York : The Macmillan Company (1926), p. 47.
26. Clifford Geertz in *Anthropological Approaches to the Study of Religion*, Michael Banton, ed., p. 4.
27. Anthony Wallace : *Religion : An Anthropological View*, p. 107.
28. Milton Yonger, J., Oberlin Colege, *The Scientific Study of Religion*, The Macmillan Company, London (1970), p. 15.
29. Edgar Sheffield Brightman, *The Problem of God*, The Abingdon Press, New York (1930), p. 164.
30. Schmidt, W., *The Origin and Growth of Religion*, tr. H.J. Rose, London : Methuen and Co. Ltd., (1935), p. 2.
31. Radha Kamal Mukherjee; '*Religious Experience*', *The Sociological Review*, April 1930, and Roots of Religion, Social Forces, Vol. VIII, p. 10.
32. Bergson; *The two Sources of Morality and Religion*, p. 175.
33. *Ibid.*, pp. 99-100.
34. *Ibid.*, p. 102.
35. Bronislaw Malinowski, *Myth in Primitive Psychology*, pp. 21, 39 London (1926).
36. *Ibid.*
37. Larousse, *World Mythology*, Ed. Pierre Grimal—London : Paul Hamlyn.

38. Bergson, *The two Source of Morality and Religion*, p. 103.
39. *Ibid.*, p. 109.
40. *Ibid.*, p. 116.
41. *Ibid.*, p. 116.
42. *Ibid.*, p. 117.
43. *Ibid.*, p. 89.
44. Susanne K. Langer, Philosophy in a New Key, p. 142—*The New American Library of World Literature*, Inc. 501, Madison Avenue, New York 22, N.Y. (1951).
45. Bergson, *The Two Sources of Morality and Religion*, pp. 89-90.
46. Colin Smith, *Contemporary French Philosophy*, Methuen and Co. Ltd., 11, New Fetter Lane, EC4—London (1964), p. 158.
47. Bergson, *The two Sources of Morality and Religion*, p. 143.
48. *Ibid.*, p. 143.
49. *Ibid.*, p. 148.
50. *Ibid.*, p. 149.
51. *Ibid.*, p. 152.
52. *Ibid.*, p. 154.
53. *Ibid.*, p. 155.
54. *Ibid.*, p. 157.
55. *Ibid.*, p. 157, *Cf.* Westermarck, *History of Human Marriage* (London, 1901) pp. 290 sqq.
56. *Ibid.*, p. 161.
57. *Ibid.*, pp. 161-62.
58. *Ibid.*, p. 171.
59. *Ibid.*, p. 172.
60. *Ibid.*, p. 172.
61. *Ibid.*, pp. 172-73.
62. Rao, Lakshmana A., *Metaphysical Psychology of Henri Bergson*—(Waltair : Andhra University Press, 1971), p. 6.
63. Lenon, P., Critical Review of Bergson's Les deux sources de la Morale et de la Religion—Mind. Vol. 41, (1932), p. 490.
64. Parkes, H.B., "*The Tendencies of Bergsonism*", *Scrutiny A quarterly Review*, Vol. IV, No. 1, 1935, Published by the Cambridge University Press—(London : Bentley House, 200, Euston Road), p. 423.

# *Chapter VI*
# Bergson as a Mystic

## 1. INTUITION IN THE TWO SOURCES OF MORALITY AND RELIGION OR BERGSON AS A MYSTIC

From the dawn of civilization man attempted to conceive the world as a whole by means of thought. Metaphysics developed, by the union and conflict of two very different human impulses, the one urging him towards mysticism, the other urging him towards science. Some men achieved greatness through one of these impulses alone : in Hume, for example, the scientific impulse reigns quite unchecked, while in Blake a strong hostility to science co-exists with profound mystic insight. But great men have felt the need of both science and mysticism. We can note that Bergson is one among them. In his *Creative Evolution* we see him founding his philosophy with his knowledge of science. Then the mystic in him was only apparent. Only in *The two Sources of Morality and Religion*, he advocates mysticism. Before Bergson, we have Heraclitus and Plato who attempted to blend both science and mysticism.

### What is Mysticism?

Mystical philosophy in all ages and in all parts of the world, is characterised by certain beliefs. "There is, first, the belief in insight as against discursive analytic knowledge : the belief in a way of wisdom, sudden, penetrating, coercive, which is contrasted with the slow and fallible study of outward appearance by a science relying wholly upon the senses. All who are capable of absorption in an inward passion must have experienced at times the strange feeling of unreality in common objects, the loss of contact with daily things, in which the solidity of the outer world is lost, and the soul seems, in utter loneliness, to bring forth, out of its own depths, the mad dance appeared as independently real and living."[1]

The mystic insight begins with the sense of a mystery unveiled. It is a hidden wisdom now suddenly become certain beyond the possibility of a doubt. The sense of certainty and revelation comes first in mysticism. Only then comes the definite belief. This belief is the result of inarticulate experience gained in the moment of insight. "The first and most direct outcome of the moment of illumination is belief in the possibility of a way of knowledge which may be called revelation or insight or intuition, as contrasted with sense, reason, and analysis, which are regarded as blind guides leading to the morass of illusion. Closely connected with this belief is the conception of a Reality behind the world of appearance and utterly different from it. This Reality is regarded with an admiration often amounting to worship; .......The second characteristic of mysticism is its belief in unity, and its refusal to admit oppostion or division anywhere. ......... A third mark of almost all mystical metaphysics is the denial of the reality of Time. This is an outcome of the denial of division; if all is one, the distinction of past and future must be illusory."[2]

Whatever tends to sharpen the demarcation between the self and the non-self and whatever isolates the subject from the Principle of Life, is anti-mystical. For the Roman Catholics mysticism is not the union of the soul with the divine Principle. For them it is superhuman knowledge. Mysticism is also defined in several other ways :

"Mysticism is a deification of man," it is "a merging of the individual will with the universal will," "a consciousness of immediate relation with the Divine", "an intuitive certainty of contact with the supernatural world."[3]

"To the mystic, Reality is not a problem but is realization itself; and Nammāḻvār, the super-mystic of Śrīvaiṣṇavism, is so deeply intoxicated by divine love that he has no other thought or feeling than that of God. Kṛṣṇa alone satisfies his organic cravings of hunger, thirst and pleasure."[4]

"The true mystic rejects the values of supernatural powers and yogic siddhis as he seeks God and only God. Visions and voices, photisms, auditions and automatisms may simulate spiritual experience but they do not lead to God; rather they lead away from Him."[5]

Almost all religions in one way or other refer to mysticism, ecstasy, supramental consciousness etc. The mystic smiles at science and plays with theology. This is because of the force he got both from his insight and inward assurance. He is all faith, all love and all vision. "Mysticism is the most primitive of feelings...... It can exist in a child, very likely in an animal; indeed, to parody a phrase of Hegel's, the only pure mystics are the brutes. When articulation fails in the face of experience; when instinct guides without kindling any prophetic idea to which action may be inwardly referred; when life and hope and joy flow through the soul from an unknown region to an unknown end, then consciousness is mystical."[6]

William James, the great American philosopher-psychologist by rendering a comprehensive service to religious psychology in his work, *The Varieties of Religious Experience* defines mysticism in it. He says that the characteristics of mysticism are four : (a) Ineffability, (b) Noetic quality, (c) Transiency, and (d) Passivity.[7]

***(a) Ineffability***

Mysticism defines expression. No adequate report of its contents can be given in words. Therefore, its quality must be directly experienced; it cannot be imparted or transferred to others. Mystical states are more like states of feeling than like states of intellect. To know the value of a symphony one must have musical ears.

### *(b) Noetic Quality*

Mystical states are similar to states of feeling. But they seem to be also states of knowledge to those who experience them. They are states of insight into depths of truth. Here, truth is unplumbed by the discursive intellect. The insights are illuminations, revelations and full of significance. As a rule they carry with them a curious sense of authority for after time.

The above two characters in the opinion of William James are the most important of mysticism. There are two other qualities which are less sharply marked, but they are usually found.

### *(c) Transiency*

Mystical states cannot be sustained for a long time. Except in rare instances, at almost an hour or two, seems to be the limit beyond which they fade. They can be reproduced in memory imperfectly.

### *(d) Passivity*

To get mystical states certain preliminary actions are prescribed by mysticism such as fixing the attention, going through certain bodily performances etc. But when the characteristic sort of consciousness has once set in, the mystic feels as if his own will were in abeyance. Sometimes he feels as if he were grasped and held by a superior power. This connects mystical states with certain definite phenomena of secondary personality, such as prophetic speech, automatic writing, or the mediumistic trance. If these latter conditions are well pronounced, however, there may be no recollection whatever of the phenomenon. It may have no significance for the subject's inner life. Mystical states are never merely interruptive. Some memory of their content always remains.

They modify the inner life of the subject between the times of their recurrence.

**Bergson and Mysticism**

According to Bergson, static religion, is, "a defensive reaction of nature against that in the exercise of intelligence which tend to depress the individual and dissolve society." Into this scheme remains belief in survival, prayer, sacrifice and the whole round of religious rites. Each of them performs a biological function of the deepest significance. But the whole system, when taken by itself apart from any deeper contact with the creative spirit of life from which it has itself emanated, remains, shut up within itself. How deliver religion[8] from this imprisonment? Round the intelligence there has remained from the first a margin of intuition. This intuition, however flickering and vague it may be, can fix and intensify so that it becomes the source of a new insight. It can guide and inspire man to a wholly new attitude to the world—a new kind of religion. This is termed by Bergson as *dynamic religion.* It differs both in its origin and its essential nature and function from the static religion. It comes into being by no continuous process of social or intellectual growth from the other; but as a revelation guaranted to chosen spirits. These privileged souls make the effort of concentration on the intuitive basis of self-consciousness and become dominated by the emotion inspired by what it finds there revealed. So, Bergson's dynamic religion having this origin has to accept *Mysticism.*

**Bergson's Self-contradiction**

Bergson says that there is absolute discontinuity between closed and open society : "Never shall we pass from the closed society to the open society, from the city to humanity, by any mere broadening out. The two things are not of the same essence."[9] But when he comes to religion he maintains that even though static religion is opposed to dynamic religion, they are not mutually exclusive : ....... "in the matter of religion, (there is) a gradual disappearance of the opposition between the static and the dynamic....."[10] Thus Bergson is obliged to contradict himself, otherwise his book could have no unity. Whether or not it is true that the élan vital is a force tending to promote universal and indivisible love, Bergson sees such a movement towards universalism as good. Religion is what sustains in man the will to live. In animals it is purely instinctive.

Bergson, to establish unity in his work, has to develop a religion which he calls dynamic on the foundation laid by static religion. In this religion, the soul, strong enough, noble enough because of its touch with the principle of static religion feels itself pervaded. It retains its own personality, "by a being immeasurably mightier than itself, just as iron is pervaded by the fire which makes it glow. Its attachment to life would hence forth be its inseparability from this principle, joy in joy, love of that which is all love. In addition it would give itself to society, but to a society comprising all humanity, loved in the love of the principle underlying it."[11] This religion which transfigures static religion aims at mysticism because it lifts the soul to another plane. Here, there is no anxious heart-searching. "Now detachment from each particular thing would become attachment to life in general."[12] Even though mysticism lifts the soul, to a pre-eminent degree, the security and the serenity which it is the function of static religion to provide."[13] Bergson has got valid reasons to arrive at mysticism : The same security and serenity which the static religion provides can also be achieved by seeing one's own life and everybody else's an intrinsically valuable and by arriving at a view of existence as something worthwhile in itself. Bergson has in mind this kind of conviction, a feeling of mystical oneness. "But we must above all bear in mind that pure mysticism is a rare essence....."[14] Bergson has to come to the above conclusion because seizing the absolute intuitively is rare. It is supremely valuable and ensures the humanity of man.

## Bergson's Criticism of Greek Mysticism

In his efforts to elaborate the kind of mysticism he has in mind, Bergson criticises the Greek mysticism. In Greece there developed two kinds of mysticism : 1. The intellectual and 2. The extra-intellectual. In the first we have the Dionysiac which merges into Orphism. In the second we have Pythagoreanism. This transmitted something of its spirit to Platonism which culminates in Alexandrine mysticism. In this category we have the mysticism of Plotinus also even though it differs from Alexandrine mysticism. Alexandrine mysticism is influenced by the Eastern thought whereas Plotinus' is not so.

### *(a) Intellectual Mysticism*

Among most uncivilized people, as among civilized people, certain ecstatic conditions are regarded as divine possession or as union with the Divine. These states are induced by means of drugs, by physical excitement, or by psychical means. Those who practise this report that they had a delightful experience beyond expression etc. In Greece, intoxication was customary in connection with established cults. Wine drunkenness was prominent in the worship of Dionysus. To the effect of the wine was added that of dancing, music, shouting, and the expectation of divine ecstacy. "But drugs are not the only physical means of producing the ecstacy dear to men of every degree of culture. Deprivations of food and sleep, isolation, even active tortures are well-known and frequent means of religious ecstacy. Rhythmic bodily movements and shouting or singing, when long continued, yield results similar in several respects to that of alcohol, stramonium, mescal, and other drugs."[15]

Bergson does not agree with this kind of mysticism because in his opinion mystical states must be attained spiritually. Attaining these states materially by artificial means and by torture through physical means is undesirable. He says, "it could just as well be brought about materially, by an inhibition of what inhibited it, by the removing of an obstacle, and this effect was the wholly negative one produced by the drug; the psychologist preferred making use of the latter, which enabled him to obtain his result whenever he wished."[16] According to Bergson this "metamorphosis of dialects into mysticism" was caused by an extra-rational force. This force caused this rational development and carried it to its culmination at a point beyond reason. "In the same way the slow, steady phenomena of sedimentation, which alone are visible to us, are the outcome of invisible seismic forces which, by heaving up at certain times the earth's crust, start the sedimentary activity in a given direction."[17]

### *(b) Extra-intellectual Mysticism*

Before going deep into this kind of mysticism, we shall see how Bergson defines 'complete' mysticism : "In our eyes, the ultimate end of mysticism is the establishment of a contact, consequently of a partial coincidence, with the creative effort of which life is the manifestation. This effort is of God, if not God himself. The great mystic is to be conceived as an individual being, capable of transcending the limitations imposed on the species by its material nature, thus continuing and extending the divine action."[18] Having the above notion about mysticism in his mind, Bergson criticises the extra-intellectual mysticism of Plotinus which according to him is incomplete. The complete mysticism is action-oriented. Any kind of mysticism which renounces action is mere contemplation according to Bergson. The mysticism of Plotinus is rejected by Bergson on this ground. As regard Plotinus, Bergson says, "it was granted to him to look upon the promised land, but not to set foot upon its soil. He went as far as ecstacy, a state in which the soul feels itself, or thinks it feels itself, in the presence of God, being irradiated with His light; he did not get beyond this last stage, he did not reach the point where, as contemplation is engulfed in action, the human will becomes one with the divine will."[19] According to Plotinus, "Action is a weakening of contemplation" which is not accepted by Bergson. So, in Bergson's opinion, mysticism was never attained by Greek thought. "No doubt it would like to have come into being; as a mere virtuality, it knocked more than once at the door. The door opened wider and wider, but never wide enough for mysticism wholly to enter."[20]

## Bergson's criticism of Oriental Mysticism

Hindu thought, is both a philosophy and a religion. It is the intermingling of the dialectical and the mystical. There is a radical distinction between the mystical and the dialectical. But the constant intermingling of these two, prevented mutually each other form attaining full maturity. India has always practised a religion similar to that of ancient Greece. Gods, spirits, rites, ceremonies and sacrifice were common both in India and Greece. These cults persisted through Brahmanism, Jainism and Buddhism. Buddhism treated men and gods as creatures of the same species, subject to the same laws of fate. This in fact agrees with Bergson's hypothesis : man naturally lives in societies. As the result of a natural function, which Bergson has called myth-making, man surrrounds himself with phantasmic beings of his own creation. He lives a life akin to his own, on a higher plane, but bound up with his own. Such is the religion Bergson regards as natural. But a Hindu mystic feels more or less distinctly that he is leaving men and gods behind him.

### *(a) Yoga : An Insufficient Form of Mystic Contemplation*

We have found that the static religion is foreshadowed in nature and the dynamic religion is a leap beyond nature. The impetus in the case of the leap of a Hindu soul is insufficient or thwarted. The Hindu soul has striven towards this impetus in different ways. One of them is of a physiological and psychological character. To trace its origin, we must refer to a practice common to Hindus and Iranians, previous, to their separation : "the recourse to an intoxicating drink which they both call *soma*. It produced a divine rapture, somewhat like that which the devotees of Dionysos sought in wine. Later came a set of practices designed to inhibit all feeling, to dull mental activity, in a word to induce states similar to hypnosis; these became systematised into the yoga."[21] According to Bergson there is nothing mystical in hypnotic states. But they can herald mysticism and pave the way for it. The practices of yoga suspend the critical functions of intelligence. This type of mysticism is only outlined. "But a more marked mysticism, a purely spiritual concentration, could utilize the yoga in its material elements, and by that very operation spiritualise it. In fact, the yoga seems to have been, at different times, and in deferent places, a more popular form of mystic contemplation, or else a complete system which included this contemplation."[22]

### *(b) Liberation of Soul : Not Complete Mysticism*

From the most remote times, the Hindu speculated on being in general, on nature, on life. But unlike the efforts of the Greek philosophers, his efforts has not led to the unlimited development of knowledge—especially to the development of science. The reason is that to the Hindu, knowledge was always rather a means than an end. "The problem for him was to escape from life, which he felt to be unremitting cruelty. And suicide would not have provided this escape, for the soul has to pass into another body after death, and this would have meant a perpetual round of living and suffering. But from the very beginning of Brahmanism, he drifted into the belief that deliverance could be won by renunciation."[23] There is no difference between Buddhism and Brahmanism in essentials. Till then it was considered by Brahmanism that life meant suffering. Buddha modified it slightly by tracing the cause of this suffering. He came to the conclusion that desire was the root cause of all sufferings. Thus Brahmanism,

Buddhism, even Jainism preach the extinction of the will to live. This is a call on intelligence. This intellectuality differs in the above three only in degrees. But on looking closer, we find that Brahmanism obtained the ultimate conviction, not by reasoning, nor by study, but through vision, passed on by him who *had* seen. In one aspect, Buddhism is more philosophical and in the other it is still more mystical. The state towards which it guides the soul is beyond joy and pain, beyond consciousness. "It is by a series of stages, and by a whole system of mystical discipline that it leads to Nirvāṇa, to the abolition of desire during life, and of Karma after death."[24] Even though Bergson accepts Buddhistic Mysticism, yet he terms it as incomplete. For Bergson says that complete mysticism "would be action, creation, love."[25]

### Mysticism without Action is Incomplete

Bergson's dynamic religion, though elaborates mostly about mysticism, we should not forget that the welfare of the humanity as a whole is the basic thing in his dynamic religion. In this regard he says that the Greek and the Indian mysticism are incomplete. The Greek mysticism which is dialectical in nature and the oriental mysticism which is mere contemplative do not convince Bergson. So, when Bergson strongly criticises the Oriental mysticism, we can note his emphasis on action.

"This burning, active mysticism could never have been kindled in the days when the Hindu felt he was crushed by nature and when no human intervention was of any avail. What could be done when inevitable famine doomed millions of wretches to die of starvation? The principal origin of Hindu pessimism lay in this helplessness. And it was pessimism which prevented India from carrying her mysticism to its full conclusion, since complete mysticism is action."[26]

Buddhism or any other school of Indian philosophy did not believe in the efficacy of human action. It had no faith in such action. According to Bergson charity is the main thing in active mysticism. Christianity which preached this kind of mysticism later on spread in India. Its influence therefore changed the mysticism of India. In this regard Bergson says, "It is perhaps to be met with in India, but much later. That enthusiastic charity, that mysticism comparable to the mysticism of Christianity, we find in a Ramakrishna or a Vivekananda, to take only the most recent examples.......... And it was industrialism, it was our Western civilization which liberated the mysticism of a Ramakrishna or a Vivekananda."[27]

The development of scientific knowledge and the inventions of machines increased the yield of the land. The products could be moved from place to place. The human suffering and the bitter poverty were won over thus by the interference of human intelligence. The Hindu mysticism which completely ignored this aspect of life and also believed sternly in the Karma theory emphasised the impossibility of such interference. It merely encouraged contemplation and renunciation. So, Bergson opines about complete mysticism thus :

> ....... "it was no longer to be driven back into doctrines of renunciation or the systematic practice of esctasy; instead of turning inwards and closing, the soul could open wide its gates to a universal love. Now, these inventions and organisations are essentially Western; it is they who, in this case, have enabled mysticism to develop to its fullest extent and reach its goal."[28]

So Bergson concluded that neither in Greece nor in ancient India was there complete mysticism. The Greek mysticism was incomplete because the impetus was not strong enough. The oriental mysticism was incomplete because its impetus was thwarted by material conditions or by too narrow an intellectual frame.

**Christian Mysticism**

Bergson supports Christian mysticism because he is

satisfied with the charity of the Christian missionaries which did excellent service to humanity. After criticising the oriental and the Greek mysticism he comes to a conclusion that only Christian mysticism is complete. In his eyes St. Paul, St. Teresa, St. Catherine of Sienna, St. Francis and Joan of Arc were complete mystics. Bergson also warns that mere hallucination, raptures, ecstasies and visions cannot be the characteristics of complete mysticism because these can occur even in the mentally retarded, in the sick and in the weak minded people. Regarding this he says, "A lunatic may think he is an emperor; he will systematically introduce a Napoleanic touch into his gestures, his words, his acts, and therein lies his madness : does it in any way reflect upon Napolean? In just the same way it is possible to parody mysticism, and the result will be mystic insanity : does it follow that mysticism is insanity?"[29]

**Identification of the Human Will with the Divine Will—True Mysticism**

Visions, raptures and ecstasies are only of secondary importance to the Christian mystics. They are only wayside incidents. They have to go beyond them to reach the goal which is the identification of the human will with the divine will.

**Image and Emotion**

Bergson clearly distinguishes between the image and the emotion when he discusses about mysticism. There is shock for the soul in its passing from the static to the dynamic, from the closed to the open and from everyday life to mystic life. When the darkest depths of the soul are stirred, there are gradations of the intensities of consciousness. These intensities can be classified from the lowest to the highest : 1. image, 2. emotion and 3. mysticism. The image is the symbolic of what is about to happen. The emotion is concentration of the soul and it is transformed into mysticism. In

Bergson's view, "the image is often pure hallucination, just as the emotion may be meaningless agitation."[30]

## The 'Will' in Mysticism

The individual and the species condition one another. In fact the natural laws demand so. But when the soul is stirred in depth, it escapes for a moment from these laws and ceases to revolve round itself. It stops, as though to listen to a voice calling. It indirectly perceives the force that moves it. It feels an indefinable presence and divines it through a symbolic vision. "Then comes a boundless joy, an all—absorbing ecstasy or an enthralling rapture : God is there, and the soul is in God. Mystery is no more. Problems vanish, darkness is dispelled; everything is flooded with light."[31] But this does not last for a long time because this is only ecstasy. The soul of the great mystic does not stop at ecstasy. He has to race forward again. However close the union with God may be, it could only be final if it were total. The distance between the thought and the object of thought is gone. "Gone the radical separation between him who loves and him who is beloved : God is there, and joy is boundless. But though the soul becomes, in thought and feeling absorbed in God, something of it remains outside; would quite naturally proceed. Its life, then, is not yet divine."[32] The soul is aware of this. The mysticism will be complete only when the will finds its way back to God.

## The Final Phase in Mysticism

Bergson gives us an example to illustrate the final phase of mysticism : A machine of wonderfully tempered steel, built for some extraordinary feat, might be in a state of being conscious of itself as it was being put together. If the machine must become a marvellous instrument, the tempered steel is subjected to the severest tests. Some of the parts are rejected and replaced by others. It would have a feeling of something lacking here and there, and of pain all over. But this is essential for the steel to become an instrument. So, also the mystic soul yearns to become this instrument. It throws off anything in its substance that is not pure enough, not flexible and strong enough, to be turned to some use by God. By now it has sensed the presence of God. It beholds God in a symbolic vision. It has been united to Him in its ecstasy. But none of this rapture was lasting, because it was mere contemplation. Action throws the soul back upon itself and thus divorced it from God. "*Now,* it is God who is acting through the soul, in the soul; the union is total, therefore final."[33] Henceforth for the soul there is a superabundance of life. There is a boundless impetus. In this state there is a calm exaltation of all its faculties. This makes it see things on a vast scale *only.* It sees things simply. This simplicity guides it through complications which it apparently does not even perceive. The step to be taken next is decided by an innate knowledge. Yet effort, endurace and persevrance remain indispensable. "But they come of themselves, they develop of their own accord, in a soul acting and acted upon, whose liberty coincides with the divine activity."[34] They represent a vast expenditure of energy. This energy is supplied from a spring which is the very source of life. In its elevation, the soul feels no pride. On the contrary his humility is great.

The mystics tell all men that the world perceived by the eyes of the body is doubtless real. But there is something else. This something is no mere possibility or probability, like the conclusion of an argument, but the certainty of a thing experienced. The mystic feels truth flowing into his soul from its fountain-head like an active force. He need not spread it because it is not by mere words that he can spread it. "For the love which consumes him is no longer simply the love of man for God, it is the love of God for all men. Through God, in the strength of God, he loves all mankind with a divine love."[35]

### Love of Humanity : The aim of Mysticism

Love towards family members, society and countrymen in a sense is selfish. When we belong to a certain group of people we ignore other groups. With family, country, humanity appearing as wider and wider circles, man must naturally love humanity as he loves his country and his family. But nature has ordained only the social group and the family group. In reality, therefore, love for one's society and family is instinctive. The social instinct would be far more likely to prompt societies to struggle against one another than to unite to make up humanity. The family and social feeling overflows to such an extent as to operate beyond its natural frontiers. But the mystic love of humanity is a very different thing. "It is not the extension of an instinct, it does not originate in an idea. It belongs neither to the sensitive nor to the rational. It is implicitly both and effectively much more. For such a love lies at the very root of feeling and reason, as of all other things. Coinciding with God's love for His handiwork, a love which has been the source of everything, it would yield up, to anyone who knew how to question it, the secret of creation. It is still more metaphysical than moral in essence."[36] With God's help the love completes the creation of the human species. Thus it makes of humanity what it would have straightaway become, had it been able to assume its final shape with the assistance of man himself. In other words its direction is exactly that of the vital impetus. This impetus is communicated in its entirety to exceptional men. They impart it to all humanity. Thus, through love, the species which is motionless once again starts its creation and hence is kept moving.

### Mechanics and Mysticism

Mysticism, by passing slowly, a part of itself from one man to another, intends to transform humanity. But there is a great obstacle on its way. Man has to earn his bread with the sweat of his brow. In other words humanity is designed for the very object of supplying him with weapons and tools, with a view to that struggle and toil. So, in these conditions it is very difficult for humanity to turn heavenwards its attention. Anyhow it achieves this goal by two different methods. The first consists in intensifying the intellectual work to such an extent, in carrying intelligence so far beyond what nature intended. The simple tool would give place to a vast system of machinery so that human activity is set at liberty. This liberty is stabilised by a political and social organisation which ensures the application of the mechanics to their true object. But the more mechancis develops, the more it reacts against mysticism. Thus, the diadic movement of both mechanics and mysticism continues. Mechanisation which is the product of the development of the human intelligence, counters the progress of mysticism. But actually it paves the way indirectly for the development of mysticism. Both of them are the contrary but complementary tendencies. If one grows, and monopolises all the room, the other will profit by this. Its turn will come again, and it will then benefit by everything which has been done without its aid. In fact, it has the chance to rectify the defects which its contrary tendency had. But this method can be used only later. In the meantime an entirely different method from the first can be followed. This consists, not in contemplating a general and immediate spreading of the mystic impetus, which is impossible. According to this method, the mystic impetus, though it is weakened, is imparted to a tiny handful of privileged souls. These souls together form a spiritual society. Each one of such society is exceptionally gifted and so they give birth to one or several others. Thus, the impetus would be preserved and continued. This goes on until there is a radical transformation in spiritual matters. The transformation is possible by the change of material conditions imposed on humanity by nature.

"Such is the method followed by the great mystics. It

was of necessity, and because they could do no more, that they were particularly prone to spend their superabundant energy in founding convents or religious orders. For the time being they had no need to look further. The impetus of love which drove them to lift humanity upto God and complete the divine creation could only reach its end, in their eyes, with the help of God whose instruments they were."[37] Therefore, their efforts are limited. They have to be convergent because God imparted to them their unity.

## Mysticism and Religion

There is little doubt that mysticism is related in one way or other to religion. But disagreement exists as to whether religion is always mystical; whether, as some put it, mysticism is at the root of every religion. If we say that religion goes always with mysticism, then the withdrawal of mysticism would result in the dying of all religions. William James, for instance, affirms, that "personal religious experience has its rot and centre in mystical consciousness."[38] Similarly, William Hocking writes of the mystics thus, "their technique which is the refinement of worship, often the exaggeration of worship, at the same time the essence of all worship."[39] Delacroix, in the preface to "Etudes d' Historie et de Psychologie du Mysticisme" says that mysticism, understood as the immediate apprehension of the divine, is "at the origin of all religion". But in an another article on "Le Mysticisme et le Religion," he says, there exist religions without mysticism."[40]

Bergson on the other hand establishes the relation between religion and mysticism based on his metaphysics. Religion is the outcome of man's intellect. So, the man of religion is being impressed by ideas. His ecstasies, when they occur, unites him to a God. But this god does not correspond to the abstract descriptions with which religion had supplied him. The teaching of religion is meant for intelligence. Anything of a purely intellectual order can be brought within the reach of all men. It is always possible to assimilate religion intellectually. But, mysticism means absolutely nothing, to the man who has no experience of it. Religion, therefore, according to Bergson, is a mere extract of mysticism being formulated by the intellect and therefore grasped by all. A doctrine invented by intellect has a poor chance of giving birth to the glowing enthusiasm, the illumination, the faith that moves mountains. "But grant this fierce glow, and the molten matter will easily run into the mould of a doctrine, or even become that doctrine ease it solidifies. We represent religion, then, as the crystalisation, brought about by a scientific process of cooling, of what mysticism had poured, while hot, into the soul of man."[41]

What the mystics experience spiritually are expressed materially by words by using intelligence through theology. These expressions are the teachings of the theologians. This is possible because theology has tapped that very current whose source is the mystical. Thus, his mysticism is served by religion. Therefore, Bergson comes to the conclusion, that "mysticism and religion are mutually cause and effect, and continue to interact one another indefinitely."[42] The task of the great mystic is to effect a radical transformation of humanity by setting an example. Through religion, all men get a little of what a few privileged souls possessed in full.

Christianity derived much from ancient religions and Greek philosophers. It is permeated with Greek philosophy, and has preserved many rites, many ceremonies and many beliefs. The new Christian religion was benefitted by its borrowings from ancient religions. Even though its tendency was in the opposite direction it kept the name (religion) to become popular. So, Bergson says, "the propagation of the mystical through religion seems to us something of the kind. In this sense, religion is to mysticism what popularisation is to science."[43]

## 2. A CRITICAL ESTIMATE

All through his philosophical career Bergson maintains

the steady and continuous unfolding of the same vital principle, the Élan Vital. "His view on morality and religion are, in the main, its logical outcome."[44] The vital principle disintegrates so that perception and intellect on the one hand, and matter and space, on the other, come into existence. This is the view held by Bergson in his earlier works. The disintegration of the vital principle is essential according to Bergson for practical purpose. Intuition and 'dissolving back into the whole' are possible only by suppressing action[45] and by making instinct disinterested.[46] But in *The two Sources,* Bergson's conception of complete mysticism, in which mystic intuition of reality and vigorous action for humanity are to exist side by side, appears to be inconsistent with that previous position. The mystic soul grasp reality through intuition and sees things simply.[47] If we accept the above view then the question arises as to how far the unbroken vision of reality can furnish the basis for a life of action, which, according to Bergson, needs the breaking up of the vital impetus, the absolute whole, into static fragments according to practical needs.

Bergson's conception of the path of complete mysticism is gradual. The final ideal is 'total' union of soul with God.[48] Until the goal is reached the mystics will 'remains outside' of God. During this period the effort is made by the will 'to find its way back to God.' This must be done through work that can take the will God-ward. 'There is boundless impetus' when the 'final phase' of total union is reached. The mystic is 'alone with Him who is Alone.' But yet the question remains how that impetus can be canalised and reduced to human activity unless the mystic again comes down to the human level? Here Bergson is unable to decide the exact status of the complete mystic. Sometimes we see him talking of the complete dissolution of the mystic in God. In this context it is necessary for him to deny personal immortality. But sometimes again he speaks like a true Christian and make the readers to come to the conclusion that Bergson is a personalist.

Another point of inconsistency is that Bergson confines open morality practically to the human level. But according to his basic philosophy the élan vital underlies all living beings. Man's love must be as wide as life. He must recognise his duties *explicitly to* the sub-human world as much as to the human. Otherwise the so-called open morality is not absolutely open.

Bergson's philosophy grew in 'the narrow intellectual frame' of Christian thought and tradition and so even the openest philosophical soul could not shake out completely racial and religious leanings. No wonder, therefore, that with all his dialectic grandeur Hegel must conclude that Christianity of the Protestant type is the supreme religious movement of the Absolute. Bergson for his part employs his intuitive insight to conclude that Christian mysticism is the completest even at the cost of self-consistency. So, Bergson's open morality has to stop at the barrier of humanity, since human duties to lower animals receive so little recognition in Christianity.

Bergson classifies all ancient Indian mysticism under the incomplete type. This betrays Bergson's ignorance of Buddha's and his followers' intense activity for the liberation of all beings. Bergson's bold but ill-informed assertion that 'Humanity had to wait till Christianity for the ideal of universal brotherhood' will be amusing to a student of Indian Philosophy. The ideal of universal brotherhood had been already emphasised well in the Upaniṣads, Jainism and Buddhism.

The Criticisms against Bergson have been chiefly due to misunderstanding caused by two kinds of defects in his style of writing : 1. His unbalanced emphasis, arising from his passionate description of things. This can be noticed in respect of his anti-intellectualism and 2. His use of words in two opposite senses, without giving the reader sufficient warning. Time, mind, consciousness, matter, etc., are used in this way creating the impression of self-contradictory assertion. The chief cause of this last defect is due to the oscillation between the two standpoints, the apparent and the real. As Bergson says sometimes, the mystic uses the words of ordinary persons, but the meanings are transfigured. Becasue of this reason, Bergson seems to assert that time is false and yet time is the only reality. But sympathetic readers would not mind these defects. They would grasp the underlying meaning of this really great thinker.

## REFERENCES


1. Russell, Bertand, *Mysticism and Logic and other Essays,* (Longmans, Green and Co., 39, Paternoster Row-London : E.C. 4, 1925), pp. 8-9.
2. Russell, Bertand, *Mysticism and Logic and other Essays,* (Longmans, Green and Co., 39, Paternoster Row-London : E.C. 4, 1925), pp. 9-10.
3. Leuba, James H., *The Psychology of Religious Mysticism* (London : Kegan Paul, Trench, Trubner and Co., Ltd., 1925), p. 1.
4. Tiruvāymoḷi, VI, 7. 1.
5. Srinivasachari, P.N., *The Philosophy of Visiṣṭādvaita*—(Madras : The Adyar Library and Research Centre, 1970), p. 439, Ch. XVIII.
6. Santayana, George., *Reason in Religion,* (Collier Books, New York, U.S.A., 1962), p. 189.
7. See James, William., *The Varieties of Religious Experience*—(Collier Books, New York, U.S.A., 1961), pp. 299-301.
8. Bergson discusses about this eleborately under the heading 'Why we use one word'? (religion) to both static and dynamic religion in his *The two Source of Morality and Religion* (pp. 181-183). Even though these two forms of religion are oposed to each other, static religion is the preliminary stage of the continuous evolution of man's religious nature. So, it is prt and parcel of the whole system. In Bergson's own words, 'Thus may arise a mixed religion, implying a new direction given to the old, the more or less marked aspiration of the ancient god, emanating from the myth-making function, to be merged into the God who effectively reveals Himself, Who illuminates and warms privileged souls with His presence.'
9. Bergson, *The two Sources of Morality and Religion,* p. 230.
10. *Ibid.,* p. 183 (bracket added).
11. *Ibid.,* p. 181.
12. *Ibid.,* p. 181.
13. *Ibid.,* p. 181.
14. *Ibid.,* p. 181.

15. Leuba, James H., *The Psychology of Religious Mysticism*—(London : Kegan Paul, Trench, Trubner and Co., Ltd., 1925), p. 11.
16. Bergson, *The two Sources of Morality and Religion*, p. 186.
17. Bergson, *The two Sources of Morality and Religion*, p. 187.
18. *Ibid.*, p. 188.
19. *Ibid.*, p. 188.
20. *Ibid.*, p. 189.
21. *Ibid.*, p. 190.
22. *Ibid.*, p. 191.
23. *Ibid.*, p. 191.
24. *Ibid.*, p. 192.
25. *Ibid.*, p. 192.
26. *Ibid.*, p. 193.
27. *Ibid.*, p. 193.
28. *Ibid.*, pp. 193-194.
29. *Ibid.*, p. 195.
30. *Ibid.*, p. 196.
31. *Ibid.*, p. 196.
32. *Ibid.*, p. 197.
33. *Ibid.*, p. 198.
34. *Ibid.*, p. 198.
35. *Ibid.*, p. 199.
36. *Ibid.*, p. 200.
37. *Ibid.*, p. 202.
38. James, William, *The Varieties of Religious Experience*, (1902), p. 379.
39. Mind, Vol. XXI, N.S. p. 39.
40. Scientia, Vol. XXI, 1917.
41. Bergson, *The two Sources of Morality and Religion*, p. 203.
42. *Ibid.*, p. 205.
43. *Ibid.*, p. 204.
44. Dhirendra Mohan Datta, The *Chief Currents of Contemporary Philosophy*, Calcutta University Press, Calcutta-6 (1916), pp. 290-91.
45. *Creative Evolution*, p. 12.
46. *Ibid.*, p. 186.
47. *The two Sources*, p. 198.
48. *Ibid.*, p. 198.

*Chapter VII*

# Shift in Bergson's Thought between 1907 and 1932 or Creative Evolution vs The two Sources of Morality and Religion

A number of books and articles have been written on the philosophy of Bergson. They are more or less half-way houses and we do not think that any of them leads us to the main philosophical doctrine, which may be described as Bergsonism. Almost all critics of Bergson have taken into consideration his monumental work, *The Creative Evolution* and those books written earlier and have drawn conclusions from these works. His last work *The two Sources of Morality and Religion* has been generally neglected. Its conclusions have been separately reviewed as 'moral and religious ideas of Bergson.' Thus, Bergson's philosophical background was isolated. There is a gap of twenty five years between his *Creative Evolution* and *The two Sources of Morality and Religion.* Our aim is to study the development of his thought that took place during these years. This study deserves serious attention.

Why was Bergson's last work neglected? It is due to the fact that Bergson here tells us a totally different story which has no resemblance to his earlier stand. If we take his last book into account, we find a thorough change in the standpoint of the philosopher. A philosopher expresses his developed mature thoughts usually in his later works. Hence, they deserve a deep study. There are reasons to believe that

*The two Sources* is the logical as well as the psychological development of Bergson's earlier works.

Now, regarding Bergson's earlier works we can summarise his thought as follows :—

1. Bergson adopts the standpoint of change as Reality. He is thus advocating the philosophy of Becoming.[1]
2. His evolution, being creative, is self-enunciated; no beginning and no end; an evolution having no source and no destiny. Élan vital is an *impersonal push* driving all the species from behind.
3. His intuition is an expansion of intellect (*Introduction to Metaphysics*); and still it is totally different in nature from intellect (*Creative Evolution*).
4. The monistic trend of the philosopher predominating (vital 'élan' being the source of every created object), he yet inclines to dualism of matter and spirit. He even admits himself to be a dualist.[2]

One of the characteristics of Bergson's philosophy is that he does not make any difference between philosophy and Religion. The very same *'élan'* of his *Creative Evolution* is conceived as manifesting itself in moral geniuses and religious mystics after breaking through matter or by triumphing over it. It works with similar force both in his philosophy and in his religion. He very often tries to maintain a link with his metaphysical doctrines put forth in *Creative Evolution*. At one place he says, "We shall not go over again what we have stated in a former work. Let us merely recall the fact that life is a certain effort to obtain certain things from raw matter that instinct and intelligence....... are two distinct means of utilizing a tool for this object."[3] After describing his mystic religion, we find him admitting that, "no doubt *we are here going beyond the conclusions we reached in Creative Evolution.* We wanted them to keep as close as possible to facts. We stated nothing that could not in time be confirmed by the tests of biology. Pending that confirmation, we had obtained results which the philosophic method, as we understand it, justified us in holding to be true."[4]

So, it is by the same that Bergson tries to arrive at moral and religious doctrines. He himself admits that the conclusions of his *Creative Evolution* were incomplete. They are completed by those of his morality and religion. "In fact, the conclusions just set out complete naturally, though not necessarily, those of our former work (*Creative Evolution*)."[5] So, in order to obtain a complete picture of Bergson's philosophy, we must combine the conclusions of his last work with those of his earlier works.

## Creative Evolution vs The two Sources of Morality and Religion

Now, let us see the significant shift of Bergson's thought between his *Creative Evolution* (1907) and *The two Sources of Morality and Religion* (1932) :

### 1. Vital impulse gets identified with Divine Love and God

In *Creative Evolution* the vital impulse is an *impersonal* push acting from the back of all species. The philosophy of *Change* is emphasised in this work and the impetus here, is indefinite and *undetermined*. This is purely metaphysical. *The two Sources of Morality and Religion* identifies the élan vital with the world ground. "It is no longer an impersonal push. It is a creative energy which can love and can desire love, which can create in purposive way."[6] We have already elaborated this point in 'A Critical Estimate', Chapter III (4).

### 2. Epistemological intellect of Creative Evolution finds application in the moral and religious spheres in The two Sources

The Élan Vital which is biological in *Creative Evolution* is used by Bergson in *The two Sources* to explain even myth, magic, morality and religion. The intellect which is abstract and mostly spoken of epistemologically takes a definite shape in *The two Sources.* Here, it is *applied* directly to social and religious spheres. But in both *Creative Evolution* and *The two Sources* the Élan Vital is evolutionary in nature. In the first it is biological evolution and in the second it is ethical and religious evolution. In the former intellect is the instrument by which matter is evolved and intuition, the faculty which can know the Reality as it is. In the latter intellect is the instrument by which habitual morality is evolved and intuition the faculty giving the higher ethic (in the case of religion the intellect is the instrument by which the traditional religion or static religion is evolved and dynamic religion through mysticism aims at the union of the soul with God or Élan Vital). See also 'A critical Estimate', Chapter V (3).

### 3. (a) There is no Source or end for Élan Vital in Creative Evolution

Bergson does not speak of any source wherefrom the Élan Vital originates. According to him it is impossible to define or trace the origin of this vital impulse because our intellect, the principle of matter is limited. He satisfies our curiosity by giving us a sort of picturesque description that this great current emerges from some central point radiating in all directions, and diverted into eddies and backwaters. At the same time, Bergson does not mention any other reality that is superior to this vital force and from which it might be taken to have originated. Thus, the vital impetus becomes sourceless, self-created and supreme Reality, *i.e.,* the source and the product are the same. Again, in his *Creative Evolution,* Bergson does not speak of any definite end or the terminating point of his Creative impetus. While criticising *Radical finalism,* he clearly mentions that creativity loses all its meaning if evolution proceeds towards a definite and ready-made plan. Then evolution becomes merely a conformity to a fixed ideal. According to Bergson, 'if life realizes a plan, it ought to manifest a greater harmony the further it advances, just as the house shows better and better the ideal of the architect as stone is set upon stone."[7] If there is a fixed goal,

Duration loses its meaning. There is no novelty or uncertainty in the creativity. Therefore, no goal can be fixed for the creative impulse. It is an unknown journey having no destination.

**(b) There is Source and end for Élan Vital in The two Source of Morality and Religion :**

When we come to *The two Sources*, Bergson adopts quite a different view. In this book, surprisingly he mentions both the beginning and the end of this Élan Vital. He declares that "this effort is of God if not God Himself."[8] Therefore, it is known from this that it is God from whom the force of creativity takes its start. God is the source of the *Élan Vital.* Bergson not only speaks of the source but also the terminating point of this creative principle : "The impetus of love that drove them (mystics) to lift humanity upto God and *complete the divine creation, could reach its end,* in their eyes, only with the help of God."[9] "They have in any case the same terminal point."[10] "They (mystics) had had to go beyond them leaving raptures and ecstasies far behind, to reach its goal, which was identification of human will with the divine will."[11] Like these, in so many other places Bergson tells us of the end of the creative effort.

After assigning a source and a destination of the creative effort, Bergson introduces several changes of vital importance in his theory of evolution. First, this effort is of God and it ends in God. The creation (of mater, *viz.*, Torpor, Instinct, and Intelligence) is a process of self-manifestation and the evolution (from matter to life) is a process of self-absorption or self-concentration of the same Absolute. Secondly, Bergson believes in a radical transformation of the humanity by the completion of evolution, *i.e.*, "tiny handful of privileged souls would form a society and societies of this kind might multiply....... thus the impetus would be preserved and continued until such a time as a profound change in the material conditions imposed on humanity by nature should permit...... of a radical transformation."[12]

## 4. Bergson admits Teleology in The two Sources of Morality and Religion

Bergson vehenmently criticises Mechanism and Teleology in his *Creative Evolution.* It is quite evident that he had a terror of any sort of teleology in his evolutionary concept because it hampers the unchecked and free movement of the Élan Vital. But later on he seems to have understood the incompatibility of such a position. So, we find him admitting in the last work that all movement of evolution takes its start from God in order to return to God. Bergson bringsforth his concept of God who undertakes creation in order to create creators; He is Love and Joy who creates in order to have besides himself lovers and joyers worthy of His Love and Joy.[13]

Bergson saves his philosophy from the charge of logical inconsistency by describing God as Love, who undertakes creation in order to create his Lovers. The very term *movement* loses all its meaning if it is not a movement towards something. "This flow that is not a flow towards anything, this movement that is not a movement by any end, is unrelieved mechanism, though it may be a mechanism of Time and not a mechanism of Space. The antidote to mechanism is not a blind movement but a purposive activity."[14] Bergson points out that this love of God for which the creation is undertake, can have no object. So, God does not become subservient to his purpose. In the musical symphony, the creation is for the sake of creation. It has no ulterior motive. Bergson's position is that creation takes its start from God and evolution merges in God.

### Immanence and Transcendence in Bergson's Philosophy

In *Creative Evolution* we see that evolution is *self-manifestation,* and *Creation is self-absorption.* The first is immanent and the second is both *transcendent* and *immanent.* One can find the difference between evolution and creation when Bergson employs *Élan Vital* for the former and God for the latter. While the transcendent Reality is 'complete' and 'eternal', the immanent Reality in the form of the *vital élan* is *'temporal'* and 'on the way of completion.' The vital flow which is pure movement is interrupted by matter because of the purpose of self-manifestation. Otheriwse there will be no evolution—Another important revolution in Bergson's philosophy of evolution is that for him evolution starts from *Life* and matter is a later product. This is a death-blow to the scientific theories of evolution because according to these theories only life is a later product and matter is primary—The immanent nature of Elan Vital which is employed by Bergson in *Creative Evolution* develops into God Who is transcendent as well as immanent in *The two Sources*. The inverted flow of the vital impulse whereby matter is created is simply a process of Reality unmaking itself—a movement for self-manifestation. His creative evolution would lose all its significance, if there is not a creativity towards some higher teleology. There must also be an endeavour to prove that the most intelligent being created by the inversion of the free activity of the supra-personal spirit has the potentiality of reasserting itself. It must also overcome the interruptions that it has encountered. Bergson appears to accept the basic truth that creation and evolution are self-manifestation and self-absorption of God. Even though, Bergson does not boldly declare this, this is the only way by which his evolutionary theory can be rendered meaningful.

**5. The Development of Intuition into Mysticism**

Bergson has given several definitions of intuition in his different books. For example, he speaks of intuition in his *Introduction to Metaphysics* strictly in an epistemological sense. His views on intuition changed later on when he wrote other books. M. Keller Stewart also finds inconsistency in his view on the relationship between intellect and intuition as expressed in *Introduction to Metaphysics* and in his other works. In fact, Bergson describes intuition only *as a way of knowing* in his *Introduction to Metaphysics*: "An absolute could only be given in intuition, whilst every thing else falls within the province of analysis."[15] Starting from his *Introduction to Metaphysics,* the mystical trend in the mind of Bergson makes its appearance almost imperceptibly and develops through *Creative Evolution,* and finally reveals itself clearly and undoubtedly in *The two Sources of Morality and Religion.*

**The Defects of Bergson's Concept of Intuition in his Earlier Works**

In his earlier works Bergson's description of intuition is negative rather than positive. In his *Introduction to Metaphysics,* he says that intuition is "a kind of intellectual sympathy by which one places himself within the object in order to coincide with what is unique in it and consequently inexpressible." Through this definition Bergson makes intuition a fabrication of intelligence. Here, intelligence is part and parcel of intuition and intuition is confined to the intellectual domain. His other definitions of intuition as *intellectual expansion or intellectual ausculation* also prove that his desire is not to distinguish intellect from intuition as separate faculties of knowledge, but distinct within the same faculty. What made others to misconceive Bergson's concept of intuition is his effort to unite intellect and intuition. He says, "A truly intuitive philosophy would realize the much desired union between science and metaphysics. While it would make of metaphysics a positive science—that is a progressive and indefinitely perfectible one—it would at the same time lead the positive sciences, properly so called, to become conscious of their true scope, often far greater than they imagine. It would put more science into metaphysics and more metaphysics into science."[16] This view of Bergson is criticised by S.K. Maitra. He asks, "We can easily understand why philosophy must put more metaphysics into science. But what justification is there in saying that philosophy must put more science into metaphysics."[17] How can the two totally different kinds of knowledge, the one moving round the object, the other entering straight-way into it, the one relative and symbolic, the other absolute and total, be united? Why should metaphysics stand in need of any science at all, if by science is meant, knowledge by analysis?

**Relative Knowledge and Limited Knowledge**

In his letter to Hoffding Bergson tries to explain what he means by intuition : "It seems to me that for everybody a knowledge which grasps an object from within which perceives it as a man would perceive himself in his apperception and his existence were but one and the same thing, is an absolute knowledge, a knowledge of something absolute. It is undoubtedly not the knowledge of the whole of the Reality; but a relative knowledge is onething and a limited knowledge is another. The first alters the nature of the object; the second leaves the object intact, but grasp a part of it only. I maintain, and I have done what I can to prove it, that our knowledge of Reality is limited, but not relative, and also that the limits may be moved further back indefinitely."[18] An intuitive knowledge which is absolute and which enters the heart of Reality can never be limited. Bergson arrives at this peculiar position due to his conception of Reality as Time. Since Time is a perpetual flow which cannot be realized fully, Bergson thinks that Reality also cannot be known fully. Our knowledge is limited because our knowledge of Reality is incomplete. This contradiction of Bergson with regard to his definition of intuition as a *'limited absolute knowledge'*, is the outcome of limiting intuition to the concept of Time.

Another contradiction that Bergson faces is, his first definition of intuition as the coincidence with what is unique in an object. If we accept the uniqueness in different objects like the realists, then it is impossible to coincide with it by means of knowledge according to the realistic point of view.

The idealists agree with the coincidence of the subject, the object and the knowledge. But they don't agree with the uniqueness in different objects. Thus both realists and idealists criticise Bergson for such a definition of intuition.

## Bergson's Realization of his Mistakes

Later on, Bergson realized the above mentioned defects in his philosophy and tried to change his view. In *Introduction to Metaphysics* itself he hints at this change. There are two utterances in this book which reveal the subconscious revelations of Bergson's mind. They are : 1. that absolute can only be given in intuition; and 2. that intuition must give us integral experience. They indicate clearly that Bergson chooses the idealistic standpoint. This improves upon his previous position that intuition coincides with the uniqueness of different objects. Thus, he changes the piecemeal and independent knowledge of separate objects into one integral experience or absolute knowledge.

## Intuition becomes Mysticism in his Last Work

The mystical trend of Bergson's mind started revolutionising his thought. He paid more attention on integral experience rather than on epistemological intuition because he found that intuition according to the definition he gave in his earlier works, was only a way of *knowing*. It served no *practical purpose*. In *Creative Evolution* itself he identified "*Creative élan*" with God. This reached its culmination in *The two Sources of Morality and Religion*. Here, Bergson identifies intuition with mystic experience. He openly advocated that true intuition is nothing but mystic experience. The main object of this mystic experience is "to lift the humanity upto God and complete the divine creation."[19] Thus, Bergson puts forth the purpose of his intuition in *The two Sources*. Intuition plays the supremely practical role; it is concerned with the highest value of life.

### 6. Intuition in The two Sources is a Rare-essence, Practical and Purposive

In *The two Sources* Bergson's assertion that intuition plays the supremely practical role reverts two of his earlier views. First, intuition in which 'there is nothing mysterious' (*Introduction to Metaphysics*), is changed into mystic experience. This is a *rare-essence,* generally found in 'diluted form'; and secondly, the non-purposive intuition of *The Creative Evolution* which had no specific task to perform is burdened with the most practical task of serving the greatest human need. Regarding his first duration we note that the commonplace and natural intuition gives place to uncommon and unnatural one. This change in his philosophy is not a sudden jump, though it is a big one. In his erlier works he maintained that intuition is the offshoot of intellect. So, it has no mysterious nature. But when he distinguishes intuition from intellect and when he maintains that intuition is *supra-rational,* he can no more maintain that it falls within the common reach of everybody. Thus, it becomes a *rare-essence.*

It is out of the above consideration that Bergson is forced to mention grades of intuition. Bergson talks of two types of mysticism : the one active and the other contemplative. The first kind of mysticism is Christian mysticism and it is perfect. The second kind of mysticism is imperfect. The Oriental and the Greek mysticisms are of the latter type. The non-practical and non-purposive intuition of *Creative Evolution* becomes practical and purposive in *The two Sources of Morality and Religion* in the supreme sense. In *Creative Evolution,* intuition is non-practical in the sense that it has nothing to do with material problems. But in *The two Sources,* intuition becomes practical in the supreme sense *viz.,* "to lift humanity upto God and complete the divine creation."

### Instinct, Intelligence and Intuition

Bergson's treatment of instinct, intelligence and intuition

sometimes confuse the readers. In his *Creative Evolution,* he maintains that intuition is instinct that has become disinterested and so instinct according to him is lower form of intuition; *i.e.,* the difference between instinct and intuition is *one of degree,* and *not of kind.* But in *The two Sources of Morality and Religion,* we see Bergson holding a different view. Here, he talks of two kinds of morality namely the closed and the open. The closed morality is based on instinct supplemented by intelligence and the open morality is based on intuition. But he says that the difference between the closed and the open morality is one of kind, and not of degree. He himself says that between these two moralities, the difference is "one of kind and not simply one of degree."[20] Between them there lies the whole distance "from finite to infinite, from the closed to the open."[21] Thus, Bergson gives up completely his previous stand, *i.e.,* instinct is but a lower stage of intuition.

**Intermediate Place of Intelligence**

Bergson's another grave mistake is his assigning an intermediate status to intelligence, keeping instinct on one side and intuition on the other. Intelligence, here, is a link between instinct and intuition, of which one is infra-intellectual and the other is supra-intellectual. He says intelligence is the "only road leading from action confined in a circle to action developing in freedom of space, from repetition to creation, from the infra-intellectual to the supra-intellectual."[22] We come to know from this that instinctive knowledge may be developed into intuitive one and the path for progress runs through the region of intelligence. This is against the two positions which he previously held. *First,* that the difference between instinct and intuition, the closed and the open morality, the static and the dynamic religion, is not one of degree but one of kind, is a point most emphasized by Bergson. But when he says that there is a way from the one to the other and that there is no discontinuity from instinct to intuition, we are compelled to believe that instinct gradually develops into intuition through the aid of intelligence. Logically, this development is one of degree because if there are two different kinds of knowledge, the passage from the one to the other is impossible. Intuition is then a matter of emergence rather than a continuous development. Secondly, if we say that intuition is a march of instinct through intelli-gence, we see that intuition becomes intellectualised. We fail to understand how intellect can give rise to intuition, being itself a creation of intuition. The static view of Reality cannot facilitate the growth of a dynamic view.

In spite of his defects in his philosophy, Bergson ultimately makes intuition an integral experience and a mystic vision which is capable of viewing the Absolute in its totality. The change that takes place in his last book has practically remodelled his philosophical doctrines. His last work is a product of his wide experience and profound insight.

**Pete A.Y. Gunter's views regarding Bergson's shift in thought between 1907 and 1932**

Regarding Bergson's change in opinions from 1907 to 1932 there are different views. When I wrote the above views to Professor Pete A.Y. Gunter of North Texas University, U.S.A., a well known interpreter of Bergson (not as an irrationalist), I got the following reply, which of course is not in agreement with the view expressed above :—

As to your contentions concerning Bergson's change in opinions from 1907 to 1932, let me reply one by one :

**1. Vital impulse gets identified with Divine Love and God**

Well, in *C.E.* (1907) Bergson had spoken of the *source* of the vital impulse as God. But in saying this he did not imply that the vital impulse and God are in any way entirely *distinct*. Source and Product are thus here *already* identified, at least in part.

Nor is this surprising. In the *Introduction to Metaphysics* he already speaks of an 'eternity' at the upper limit of duration, and states that there is a continuity of duration leading from this eternity to 'materiality.'

**2. The sourceless and endless creative 'clan' is spoken of as originating from and culminating in God**

But the question remains as to whether this origination involves *absolute determination.* Does Bergson's God stamp out the products of his thought as an engineer constructs a machine? Or does Bergson's God attempt, as Bergson phrases it, to 'create creators'? For Bergson, even the matter (in fact, matter-energy) of the physicists has an undetermination of its own. Why should it be strange that man does?

**3. Intellectual Intuition Turns into Mystic Experience**

But *throughout* Bergson's writings he distinguishes intuition *par excellence,* the intuition of the genius, with intuition *par ordinaire,* to which we all have access. What is strange about his continuing this distinction in *The two Sources?* The great mystics are the religious geniuses. The rest of us are less open to the mystic insight, and our intuitions are more 'diluted'.

**4. Non-purposive and non-practical intuition becomes 'Purposeful and Supremely Practical'**

If I am correct, Bergson's intuition, though it is sought *for itself and with no desire for practical ends,* nonetheless expresses itself in terms which are of the greatest practical interest. This is one of the fundamental 'paradoxes' of Bergsonism : that to be pragmatic we must resist ordinary pragmatic ends. His treatment of the sciences and technology makes this perfectly clear. And the failure to see this has led to the silliest misinterpretations of his thought...... But *The two Sources* is the only book which Bergson devotes to social theory. No doubt, then, it should be *the* book in which he concentrates on the *broadly social* uses of intuition.

### 5. The common-place and not at all Mysterious Intuition becomes a Rare-essence

See the reply to Ē 3. above, which belongs here. To reply to Ē 3 here, would take a great deal of time, and would involve much analysis of texts. Let me say briefly here only that the basic characteristics of intuition are not so much changed between *C.E.* and *The two Sources.* The passion, direction, creativity, energy indentified with intuition in *The two Sources* are equally identified with it elsewhere.

As to Flewelling, in the article, which you have quoted he is having to 'eat crow' for his past book about Bergson, in which he was extremely critical. I do not find it strange that he should have tried to make *The two Sources* radically distinct from Bergson's previous books, seeing that he had, concerning those previous books, said so many harsh things. (Incidentally, if Bergson *is* a personalist, this makes it all the more unlikely that he was a theological determinist. A personalist admits several persons, not just *one.* And he will never concede that all persons (human beings) are controlled by one Big Person (God).

Finally, since for Bergson God is *Becoming,* recourse to God in Bergson's metaphysics does not involve toward regression on Bergson's part toward a principle of *Being a la Plato,* à la Parmenides..........."[23]

I do not want to comment or criticise Gunter's views expressed above. I have merely given his views and leave them to the readers to draw conclusions by comparing them with the points which we have already discussed earlier.

### 6. Shift in Bergson's thought regarding the Roman Catholic Church

Professor Gunter agrees with us regarding Bergson's shift of thought concerning the Roman Cathologic Church. This is the culmination of his shift in thought. Bergson lived on into his eighties. Due to ill-health, he became more and more retiring. So, his last book represented a victory over pain. When he died (January 5th, 1941) at the age of 82, soon after an act of courage, his will was found to contain a request:

"My reflections have led me closer and closer to Catholicism, in which I see the complete fulfillment of Judaism. I would have become a convert had I not seen in preparation for years a formidable wave of anti-Semitism which is to break upon the world. I wanted to reamin among those who tomorrow will be persecuted. But I hope that a Catholic priest will consent, if the Cardinal Archbishop of Paris authorizes it, to come to say prayers at my funeral."[24]

This is a deep transformation as far as Bergson is concerned because he had been all the time advocating biological evolution in which Élan Vital was the main concept. Apart from Bergson's declining health there were also political reasons which made Bergson revive his earlier views on the Roman Catholic Church. The scientific inventions which did more harm than help in the first world war to the people of the West and the growing uncertainty in the minds of the people about their future drew the attention of Bergson. He felt the need for the religious and the spiritual values in life. Ian W. Alexander also supports our view that Bergson turned to Catholoicism in his later years. He says, 'Bergson's relations with Christianity and with Catholicism in particular have lately been clarified."[25] Alexander cites Bergson's wife's letter as a proof for this. In a letter to Emmanuel Mounier, published in the Gazette de Lausanne on 9th September, 1941, Madame Bergson has revealed that from the *Deux Sources* onwards her husband considered Catholicism with an increasing sympathy.'[26] Ben-Ami Scharfstein, when referring to Bergson's inclination towards Catholicism says, "It is now our task to trace the development of Bergson's thought, from its initial affirmation of freedom until its final glorification of Christian mysticism, and even beyond the glorification, to near-union with Catholic thought."[27]

This deep transformation of Bergson cannot be appreciated unless we know his family background : Bergson's great grand-father, Samuel Zbitkower, was a rich Warsaur Jew with typical beard and earlocks. He dressed in a long silken cloak gathered in by a woven girdle. Zbitkower means 'from Zbitkow'. He was a merchant. He later turned to selling grain. He shipped grain by raft down the Vistula to Danzig. He was given official 'privilege' of dwelling in localities forbidden to Jews. So, his wealth increased : he established sawmills, bought houses, estates and forests. He was so rich that he was a benefactor to his poor fellow Jews.

Bergson's grand-father, Berek son of Samuel, was born in 1764. He was also a privileged Jew. He even increased his father's wealth. In accordance with the prevailing custom of rich Jews, he was also rich in charity like Samuel.

Berek had three sons, Berek-sons, or Bergsons, Jacob, Leopold, and Michael. Michael's son was to become the famous philosopher, *i.e.*, Henri Bergson. Leopold's son, also named Michael became the hard-working leader of the Warsaw Jewish community.

Bergson's father, born in 1818, loved music. He was even himself a composer. In fact, he was the first to popularise the composition of Chopin in Europe, carrying them to France, Italy, Belgium, and England. He was head of the conservatoire in Brussels for many years. He married Katherine Levinson, an English Jewess. In his old age he settled in London, where he died in 1898. He left his widow to survive him by many years. The brother of Henri Bergson was an English author of little fame. He lived in London and wrote anonymously. Henri, born in France, was a Frenchman. However, he was always close to England. When he became famous his opponents attacked his philosophy of Jewishness. But Bergson retorted them and said, "I am a Jew, and my ideas are condemnable because they are Jewish. I should willingly admit them to be such, but the misfortune is that I am not at all of it. Or rather, I am certain of profound obligation to only two or three philosophers, none of whom is Jewish; Plotinus, Maine de Biran, and somewhat to Ravaisson."[28]

Most of the Jews born French were assimilated. So, when Bergson was queried about the Jewish problem and Zionism, he answered as a typical, assimilated French Jew. He said, "To us French people this question seems paradoxical. We are so completely assimilated. If there were a new Zion I do not think many Jews would go there........ I believe the Jewish queston will be solved when the Jewish people will have attained equal rights in the countries where they have been persecuted. And the sooner that is attained the better for the Jews of course, and also for the countries where they live."[29]

The step to embrace Catholicism after complete assimilation was not so great; but from Samuel Zbitkower or from Berek, it was tremendous. Bergson's inclination towards Catholicism is not a sudden development. It developed gradually from the time of his grand-father. As he grew older his attachment towards Catholicism increased. So, Élan Vital (through which he became popular) did not attract him any longer. Both Jewish and Catholic roots can be found in Bergson's *The two Sources of Morality and Religion* due to his above background. In this work he praises the Prophets of Israel. But he subordinates them to the Catholic mystics.

It is true Bergson gave us a different view of reality and intuition in his book *The two Sources of Morality and Religion.* But if we are to take this view seriously, we have to recast the whole of his earlier views. For example, we have to discard the view of reality as pure duration or pure flow. If God as Love is the ultimate Reality, then such a Reality cannot be spoken of as mere unimpeded flow. God as Love is rich in qualities whereas the unimpeded flow is qualitiless. In that case the course of evolution will not be a mere floating on a shoreless sea. It will be a definite movement guided by definite ends. Again, intuition will cease to be a mere flash revealing nothing. It will become a steady stream of light revealing a fundamental unity because the mystic's vision does not exhibit diversity.

Bergson's last book shows that he himself perceived certain defects of his philosophy which led to a new enunciation of some of its leading principles. Perhaps due to old age and failing health, he could not give a reorientation of his philosophy in the light of this new enunciation. But when we compare his contribution to philosohy, the defects are negligible. It is no small thing to have created a revolution in the methods of philosophy. The method of intuition with all its faults is a direct challenge to the method of logical reasoning which dominated the whole field of philosophy for many centuries. Centuries old habits of thinking received a rude shock at the hands of Bergson's new philosophy. His irresistible dynamism gave a death-blow to both realism and idealism : "Both alike were static, the one imprisoning us in a fortress of mechanism, the other confinig us within the four walls of a ready-made logic. Escape from both these prisons was what the human soul cried for, and it obtained it in the philosophy of Bergson."[30]

## SUMMARY

The following is the Bergson's shift of thought between his *Creative Evolution* (1907) and his *The two Sources of Morality and Religion (1932)* in a nutshell :

1. The Vital impulse (of *Creative Evolution*) gets identified with Divine Love and God in *The two Sources of Morality and Religion.*
2. The epistemological intellect of *Creative Evolution* finds application in the moral and religious spheres in *The two Sources.*
3. The sourceless and endless Élan Vital of *Creative Evolution* finds source and end in *The two Sources.*
4. Bergson admits Teleology in *The two Sources of Morality*

*and Religion* whereas he vehemently opposes any kind of Mechanism or Finalism in *The Creative Evolution.*

5. Epistemologial Intuition becomes Mysticism in his last work.
6. Intuition in *The two Sources* is a rare-essence, practical and purposive.
7. Shift of Bergson's thought is noticed in *The two Sources* with regard to the Roman Catholic Church.

## REFERENCES

1. See A.C. Bhattacharya, *Sri Aurobindo and Bergson;* Jagabandhu Prakashan, Ramakrishna Bhavan, Gyanpur (Varanasi) 1972, pp. 5-6, and for the discussion that follows this.
2. *Cf.* The English Introduction to Bergson's *Matter and Memory.*
3. Bergson, *The two Sources of Morality and Religion,* p. 107.
4. *Ibid.,* p. 244 (Italics not in the original).
5. *The two Sources of Morality and Religion,* p. 245.
6. Ralph Tyler Flewelling, '*Bergson and Personalism,*', p. 89 (The Personalist, Vol. XIV, 1933).
7. Bergson, *The Creative Evolution,* pp. 108-9.
8. Bergson, *The two Sources of Morality and Religion,* p. 209.
9. *Ibid.,* p. 225 (Italics not in the original).
10. *Ibid.,* p. 335.
11. *Ibid.,* p. 218 (Italics not in the original).
12. Bergson, *The two Sources of Morality and Religion,* p. 225.
13. *Cf.* Bergson's *The two Sources of Morality and Religion,* p. 243.
14. S.K. Maitra's article, '*The Problem of Reality,* published in the *Philosophical Quarterly,* Jan., 1938.
15. Bergson, *Introduction to Metaphysics,* p. 6.
16. *Ibid.,* p. 63.
17. S.K. Maitra, Third Article on '*The Philosophy of Henri Bergson*', Published in *Review of Philosophy and Religion,* Jan., 1942.
18. Quoted in J. Chevalier's *Henri Bergson,* pp. 85-86.
19. Bergson, *The two Sources of Morality and Religion,* p. 225.
20. *Ibid.,* p. 24.
21. *Ibid.,* p. 24.
22. *Ibid.,* p. 56.
23. I am extremely grateful to Professor Pete A.Y. Gunter for his kind reply. The letter is dated 22nd February, 1977.
24. Quoted from J. Maritain, *Ransoming the Time,* p. 101, note.

25. Ian W. Alexander, *Bergson, Philosopher of Reflection*, p. 69, (Bowes and Bowes London).
26. Mme Bergson's letter is reproduced in the Avant propos to Essais et Temoignages.
27. Ben-Ami Scharfstein, *Roots of Bergson's Philosophy*, p. 102 (*Columbia University Press*, New York, 1943).
28. From the reminiscences of Gilbert Maire, in his book, *Bergson mon maitre*, (p. 222).
29. From an interview by Herman Bernstein, held in 1912, and recorded in his collection, *With Master Minds* (pp. 105-6).
30. S.K. Maitra, Third article on '*The Philosophy of Henri Bergson*,' Review of Philosophy and Religion, Vol. 11, Jan., 1994.

## *Chapter VIII*

# Recent Trends in Bergson's Philosophy

The primary goal of this chapter is to over come the 'erasure' of Bergson from post - Kantian philosophy. "Perhaps never before", muses James W. Felt, "has so influential a philosopher so abruptly expired within the profession at large. The Bergson who in 1913 occasioned one of New York City's first traffic jams does not rate today even a bibliographic reference in most new books discussing freedom and determinism — yet this was an area in which Bergson made original and definitive contributions". One reason for this professional demise, Felt argues is Bergson's uncompromising concern with real metaphysical issues. It would be easy to add others: the 'positivistic avalanche', the rise of phenomenology (with its promise of 'scientific' methods) and the cultural disaster. Whatever the reasons it is clear that for the most part Bergson's Philosophy, once illustrious and popular, has now been marginalized. Though the logical positivistic and the analytic philosophies dominated the academic fields in the later half of the twentieth century, the post-modern thinkers have marginalized both logical positivism and linguistic philosophy. The chosen areas of post-modern thinkers are Aesthetics, Art Literature and Science. Philosophy of Science of the contemporary thinkers such as Karl Popper and Thomas Kuhn focused more on the *methodology* rather than on the contents of science.[1] Henri Bergson went beyond methodology and his ideas influenced many thinkers such as Einstein, C.G. Jung, Heidegger, Michael Polanyi, A.N. Whitehead, Stephen Toulmin, Milic Capek, Lewis S. Fever, Lewis Wolpert, Brian C. Goodwin and Morril Cohen. The 'deconstruction' of Derrida, the 'post-structuralism' of Foucault, the 'falsification' of Karl Popper and the 'paradigm-shift' of Thomas Kuhn differ essentially from Henri Bergson. Whereas Henri Bergson contributed originally to Reality, Life, Space, Time Cosmology and Consciousness the others focused either on 'methodology' of science or on conceptual analysis. Recent trends in Bergson's philosophy include the relevance of Bergson to the Philosophy of Science, Globalisation, post-modernism and a probe into Bergson's shifts of thoughts as revealed from his works. In the previous chapters an attempt was made to probe into Bergson's shift of thought between his *Creative Evolution* (1905) and *The two Sources of Morality and Religion* (1932). There are too more major shits in Bergson's thought: (1) the shift in his thought between *'Time and Free Will'* and *'Matter and Memory'* and (2) that between *'An Introduction to Metaphysics'* and *'The Creative Mind'*.

**Time and Free will vs Matter and Memory**

Bergson speaks sometimes as a dualist admitting two ultimate realities : matter and mind. Sometimes he speaks, like a monist, insisting that all our actions spring from one common centre or one ultimate force of consciousness. In his *Time and Free Will*, Bergson says that events take place in time in the *internal world* as well as in the *external*. The states in the mind succeed one another. But things in the *external world* are perceived as *simultaneous*. They extend in space, outside one another and *present* all *together*. He defines simultaneity as the intersection of time and space: it is the connecting link between duration and space, for each moment of duration "can be brought into relation with a state of the *external world* which is contemporaneous with it, and can be separated from the other moments in consequence of this very process".[2] Thus, external world is the simultaneous togetherness of many objects existing side by side. The successive states of the external world are the different simultaneous presentations of the world arranged successively by the mind. Here Bergson does not reduce the *external world* to mind to accept it as the only reality, nor he reduces the mind to the external world to accept it as the only reality. For him, both the internal and the *external world* exist simultaneously. But when we come to his *Matter and Memory*, we see him rejecting any kind of dualistic hypothesis of psycho-physical parallelism. Here, he says that mind is not dependent on matter and consciousness is neither produced by, nor even adequately expressed by, changes in the brain and the body. 'Memory' or 'Consciousness' is the basic Reality which uses *brain as a selector rather than a generator of ideas.* Thus, Bergson explains away the external world which is contrary to the view he held in his *'Time and Free Will'*.

**An Introduction to Metaphysics vs The Creative Mind**

In Bergson's earlier writings (*An Introduction to Metaphysics*) intellect and intuition are two different faculties of knowing a thing. Intuition goes in the very direction of life; intellect goes in the inverse direction. Intuition is absolute and to think intuitively is to think in duration. Intelligence is symbolic and relative. It starts from the immobile and reconstructs movement as best at can with immobilities in juxtaposition. Intuition starts from the movement and perceives it as reality itself. It sees in immobility only an abstract moment a snapshot taken by our mind, of a moment. But Bergson shifts his thought regarding the relation between intellect and intuition to a different position in his *'The Creative Mind'* . His outlook changes as to consider intellect and intuition to be complementary rather than contradictory to each other. He says, "in every line that I have written there is assurance to the contrary: my intuition is reflection".[3] In the same work he adds that "intuition will be communicated only by the intelligence".[4] For "......... as soon as we have intuitively perceived the true, our intellect recovers itself, corrects itself, intellectually formulates its error. It has perceived the suggestion; it furnishes the verification".[5] Here intuition is described by Bergson not as anti-scientific and one can even, conclude that in *'The Creative Mind'*, he tries to bridge the gulf between science and philosophy which he himself created in his *'An Introduction to Metaphysics'*.

**Bergson and Post-Modernism**

Post modernism is described as a set of critical, strategic and rhetorical practices employing concepts such as difference, repetition, the trace, the simulacrum and hyper reality to destabilize other concepts such as presence, identity, historical progress, epistemic certainty and the univocity of meaning. Jean-Francois Lyotard gets the pride of place for introducing the term 'post modernism'. It covers a wide variety of disciplines such as art, architecture, music, film, literature, sociology, science, communication, fashion and technology. Though philosophical post-modernism begins with Kant's "*Copernican revolution*" that is, his assumption that 'things in themselves' can not be known others who are mentioned as post-modern thinkers are Kierkegaard, Marx, Nietzsche, Martin Heidegger, Lyotard, Michel Foucault, Deleuze, Jaeques Derrida, Jean Bandrillard, Vattimo, Jurgen Habermas and Richard Rorty. Though Henri Bergson contributed originally to sociology, religion and science his name is not included in the list of post-modern thinkers.

Bergson's views on Space, Time, Energy, Evolution and Intuition had influenced many thinkers of the west. It was not an accident that Albert Einstern rejected the Newtonian Theory of Space and Time. The Newtonian Theory that 'Space and Time are absolute' was not acceptable not only to Einstern but also to Bergson. According to Bergson Space and Time are inseparable. Bergson stated that Einstern's theory of relativity was founded on a brilliant 'intuition' and 'Motion' could be accepted without pre-supposing a single one of the motionless stage back drops of the Newtonian system. And the acceptance of motion, of process of duration leads to an insight into physical nature. Bergsonian interpretation of 'matter' was similar to that of quantum physics. Thus Lewis Fever, in his *Einsterin and the Generations of Physics,* argues that Louis de Broghi was led to develop his "wave theory of matter" [which formed the bridge (1926) between the earlier quantum theory of Bohr and the later theories of Heisenberg and Schrodinger] through the direct inspiration of Bergson's Philosophy. De Broglie's own essay compares Bergson's insights into the nature of matter and of causality to those employed by contemporary quantum physics.[6] Milic Capek in his *Bergson and Modern Physics* analyses twentieth century physics in the light of Bergson's theory of matter: Both relativity and quantum physics must be interpreted, as denying the existence either of instantaneous, homogeneous space or of an entirely 'extended' material world.[7] And that is precisely what Bergson, on his own terms, denied. Bergson accepts many of the important conclusions of relativity theory, including Einstein's denial of absolute space, the ether and absolute motion, and the relativistic affirmation of the speed of light,[8] prior to the revolutions in 20th Century Physics, Bergson foresaw the coming conceptual upheaval and was able to suggest some of its general features. He could foresee the revolutions in physics and other sciences through his opposites: intuition-intelligence, duration-space and creativity-automatism. In each of his books the basic effort is to transcend our visual, static, 'spatial' schemes and rediscover the more fluid, dynamic reality which otherwise escapes us, whether in ourselves, in non-living matter, in living things or in human societies. According to Bergson Einstein's denial of Newtonian concept of matter, Motion and Space was an attempt to overcome the 'static' scheme and rediscover the dynamic and fluid reality.

**Bergson and Mathematics**

As post modernism includes the interpretations science, Bergson's view on infinitesimal calculus based on his philosophy of change are relevant to post-modern ideas. *Jean Milet's Bergson et le calcul infinitesimal: Ou, La raison et le temps* sets aside a widespread belief concerning Bergson, namely, that he was not "mathematically trained".[9] Bergson shared with his contemporary mathematicians such as F. Evellin and Constantin in the importance of the infinitesimal calculus in the understanding of modern mathematics. He said that time and motion could be explained through intuition. Initially, intuition was to be conceived in terms of the infinitesimal calculus. According to Bergson intuition has always been an attempt to 'catch the bind in flight' : to follow motion, duration, change of all kinds without deforming them. The existence of duree (duration) could be established both by a phenomological appeal to direct experience and by an appeal to the infinitesimal calculus, whose function is to describe acceleration or, as Bergson put it the 'tendency to change'. Bergson insisted that the connection between this direct experience and calculus was very close. It was through this idea of acceleration that the calculus was created. Bergson argued that Galileo was able to arrive at that most fruitful of ideas, by rescuing thought from the two Aristotelian immobilities, 'high' and 'low' by which motion was then thought to be explained. Aristotle to fix his immobilities observed the behaviour of bodies on the inclined plane throughout their fall, The calculus, based on Galileo's insight, made it possible for the human intellect, for the first time to deal with continuous change without "spatializing" or otherwise freezing it.[10] Milet' s work shows that mathematical conceptions were at the source of Bergon's Philosophy.

**Bergson and Modern Cosmology**

According to Bergson when there is 'tension', 'matter' and 'consciousness' confront each other for further creation. When the tension is released there is 'detension' and there is increasing uniformity and homogeneity of matter. In the increasing detension there is increasing entropy. In his *Creative Evolution,* he connects 'detension' and 'entropy' in a psychological model to explain the genesis of matter: "Let us seek, in the depths of our experience, the point where we feel ourselves most intimately within our own life. It is into pure duration that we then plunge back, a duration in which the past, always moving on, is swelling unceasingly with a present that is absolutely new. But, at the same time, we feel the spring of our will strained to its utmost limit. We must by a story recoil of our personality on itself, gather upon past which is slipping away, in order to thrust it, compact and undivided, into present which it will create by entering".[11]

**Suppose this thought experiment is pursued in the opposite direction**

"Now let us relax the strain, let us interrupt the effort to crowd as much as possible of the past into the present. If the relaxation were complete, there would no longer be either memory or will we get a glimpse of an existence made of a present which recommences unceasingly—devoid of real duration, nothing but the instantaneous which dies and is born again endlessly. Is the existence of matter of this nature?

Not altogether, for analysis resolves it into elementary vibrations the shortest of which are of very slight duration, almost vanishing, but not nothing".[12]

Like mind, matter, having lost its creative momentum, "detends" towards increasing spatiality, externality and repetition. Bergson must therefore be interpreted as proposing an 'expanding universe', in which the components of matter become increasingly displaced in relation to each other.[13] Bergson not only speculates the structure of the physical universe (cosmology) but also tries to find its source as well (cosmogony). Whence come all the seemingly inexhaustible supplies of physical energy which support the continual 'degradation' of matter. Conceivably energy might be drawn from other parts of the universe to sustain the increase in entropy. This amounts to suppose the existence of a spatially infinite universe, which Bergson rejects. According to Bergson, "......... the universe is not made, but is being made continually. It is growing, perhaps indefinitely, by the addition of new worlds".[14] Or, more figuratively: "So, from an immense reservoir of life, jets must be gushing out unceasingly, each of which is a world".[15] Bergson concludes that an ultimate explanation of the creation of matter must involve theological questions[16] and therefore, it is enough for him simply to explore the structure of a universe sustained by the continual appearance of new matter with its confines.

The above views of Bergson are in agreement with the 'steady-state' cosmological theory. Defenders of the steady-state cosmology hold that matter is being created throughout the universe, whose vacated regions gradually fill with newly formed galaxies. The continuous creation of matter ensures that the galactic population of any region of space must remain constant, and the universe thus retain a 'steady-state'.[17] The rival theory of the 'steady-state' is evolutionary theory. Followers of evolutionary cosmological models say that the universe, in expanding, passes through states of decreasing density as its constituent galaxies become increasingly displaced. Ultimately (assuming that the universe does not there at some points pass into a state of collapse occasioned by the ascendance of gravitatorial over expansive forces) the cosmos must reach a state of dispersion so complete that light signals from different galaxies will not reach other galaxies and each will inhabit a night of darkness alone.[18]

**Bergson and Carl Gustav Jung**

Henri Bergson's psychologically-inclined philosophy and C.G. Jung's philosophically-inclined analytical psychology can be analyzed for their similarities. Though Bergsonian movement was eclipsed after World War I, it caused an immense impact on the thinkers of the West. C.G. Jung was one of the thinkers who was influenced by Bergson's elan vital, intuition and creativity. Jung has stated clearly the similarities which he perceived between his views and Bergson's.

In 1914 he stated :

> "I realize that my views are parallel with those of Bergson and that in my book (The Psychology of the Unconscious) the concept of the libido which I have given is a concept parallel to that of *elarn vital*; my constructive method corresponds to his intuitive method. I, however, confine myself to the psychological side and to practical work. When I first read Bergson a year and a half ago I discovered to my great pleasure everything which I had worked out practically, but expressed by him in consummate language and in wonderfully clear philosophical style".[19]

The date of this admission is important, since it locates Jung's acquaintance with Bergson's philosophy at the time

Jung was struggling to free himself from his collaboration with Sigmund Freud. As is widely known, it was the libido-concept which increasingly divided Jung and Freud. For Freud, libido was primarily sexual; but Jung increasingly resisted this point of view, insisting that sexuality is one component of psychic energy, but not its essence.[20] When Jung speaks of an "onward urging, living libido[21] or of an "active fructifying (upward striving) form of the libido"[22] we find ourselves in the presence of an elan vital. During the period 1913-1920 Jung specifically equates Bergson's ideas with his own concepts of instinct,[23] intuition,[24] the function of the human intellect,[25] reaction-formation[26] and introversion-extroversion.[27] His treatment of mechanism and finalism as categories of thought during these years is notably similar to Bergson's.[28] The instructive personality as one of the basic psychological types is the idea of Jung derived from Bergson. Like Bergson, Jung connected intuition with future-oriented speculation.[29] Whatever its actual influence Bergson's *Creative Evolution* played a role in the development of Jungian concepts such as the archetypes, individuation, the collective unconscious and intuition. What was 'collective unconscious' to Jung, was 'collective biological memory' to Bergson. When a mystic or an artist is seized by an archetype, as Jung puts it, we do not have to visualize him in the grip of a crystallized, abstract form. Rather he is grasped by fundamental energies which it is his task to express in novel forms. Like Bergson, then Jung describes the artists' and the mystics creativity as the crystallization of an underlying psychic flux or stream. For both thinkers, possibility is not 'ahead of' us, in a set of clearly marked out ideal characteristics. Such a view is rejected by them as an unrealistic form of "finalistic" teleology. Rather, for both Jung and Bergson, possibility is "behind us", in a set of biological conditions stemming from the past. Self-realisation is for Bergson inevitably differentiation, the divergence from a shared trait to the development of traits uniquely defining an individual. Like Jung, Bergson too sees human history as a process of differential self-realisation. It can not be denied that Jung derived his dynamic psychiatry from the philosophy of Bergson. There is an extraordinarily close agreement of these two thinkers on many basic points—an agreement that historians of psychology have overlooked. This fundamental agreement should be useful when it comes to looking at creativity in Jung's thought.

**Bergson and Heidegger**

Temporalism and philosophy of life were powerful movements during the beginning of the 20th Century. Henri Bergson's *Time and Free Will* and Matter and *Memory*, Edmund Husserl's *Phenomenology of Internal Time Consciousness*, Martin Heidegger's *Being and Time* and Herbert Spiegelberg's. *The Phenomenology Movement* reveal to us the importance given to Time and Consciousness in the early part of 20th century. Bergson's birth is separated from Heidegger's by exactly thirty years: 1859 to 1889. More interestingly, Heidegger's birth very nearly coincides with the publication of Bergson's *Time and Free Will*. The identification of "tempora-lity" as the essence of human-being preceded Heidegger's *Being and Time* (1927) by well over three decades. There were specific points of contact between Heidegger and Bergson on the problem of time and life. Edmund Husserl's *Phenomenology of Inner Time Consciousness* edited by Heidegger and published first in 1928 refers to "Stream of Consciousness" and the "memory of the present", a phrase coined by Bergson.[30] Since Husserl was fully aware of Bergson's views on Time and Consciousness Heidegger would have learned through Husserl's work. In reading Heidegger's early essay on time and history one is struck by his sharp distinction between "qualitative and homogeneous" time,[31] for it is in Bergson's *Time and Free Will* that this contrast is delineated for the first time in the history of philosophy and in precisely these terms. Though Heidegger has not mentioned Bergson any where in the essay when we read the text there is a virtual congruence between the two thinkers.[32] Not only does Heidegger sharply oppose quality and quantity, the heterogeneous and the homogeneous in the same manner as he opposes time to space, holding that they are "opposites"[33]; he opposes the "intrinsic flow" of time "to the mathematically segmented time scale"[34], he describes "frozen time" as a "surface"[35] Readers of both *Time and Free Will* and *Matter and Memory* will be familiar with the manner in which Heidegger, in dealing with the nature of historical as opposed to physical time, describe the past as entering into the present, being absorbed by it, thus making creativity possible.[36] However, Heidegger asserted that Bergson's concept of duration was derived from Aristotle: "In its results, Bergson's view in accord with Hegel's thesis that space 'is' time, in spite of the very different reasons they have given. Bergson merely says the reverse: that time (temps) is space, Bergson's view of time too has obviously arisen from an Interpretation of the Aristotelian essay on time. Bergson prefaces his analysis of time with an analysis of number. Time as Space is quantitative succession. By a counter orientation to the conception of time, duration gets described as qualitative succession".[37]

However, in 1975 Heidegger published *The Basic Problems of Phenomenology* in which his opinion differs in tone from those asserted earlier. In this work his concept of temporality is closer to some basic Bergsonion concepts. In his interpretation of Bergson in *Sein* and *Zeit*, parts I and II, Heidegger makes it clear that he wishes to defend temporality against three Bergsonion errors. First, he wishes to defend the ordinary notion of clock time against Bergson's attack[38]. Second a matter closely related to the defence of clock-time- he wishes to deny Bergson's contention that quantitative time is an externalization, into space, of qualitative time.[39] Third, he wishes to show that the true phenomenon of temporality is the movement of time *from the future into the past*, not the movement (as Aristotle, Hegel and Bergson would have it) out of the past into the future. Though Bergson denied "clock" time in his *Time and Free Will* he defends it in his *Duration and Simultaneity* (1922). In his *Matter and Memory* he reverses what he had stated in *Time and Free Will* and adds that nothing in the outer world corresponds to our inner duration. Heidegger and Bergson deny the mathematical interpretation of becoming. Heidegger accepts two kinds of temporality: the temporality of Dasein and primordial temporality. The temporality of Dasein is the temporality of dates, specific happenings which Heidegger defends against Bergsonian attack. However, when Heidegger says that the temporality of Dasein is derived from the "Primordial Temporality" his view is closer to Bergson' s externalization of basic qualitative temporality. For both Bergson and Heidegger, the "true" mode of knowing and the "true" mode of being are disguised and hidden from us. The tension between opposites, for both grounds the concrete dialectic which is the only source of valid insight. Aristotle's explanation of natural processes involving potentiality and actuality is rejected by Heidegger as inconsistent with freedom. Since "actuality" is followed by "potentiality", it is a kind of determinism from the past to the present. According to Heidegger events come towards us from the future and temporality is thus proceeding from the future towards the past. It is interesting to see that for Bergson, who also seeks to found a concept of authentic freedom, present creativity creates a negatively vectored temporality. This is the meaning of his seemingly paradoxical assertion, in his *Time and Free Will,* that a free act is "an effect which produces its own causes"[39] present freedom recasts the out come and the significance of at least our own immediate pasts. Besides the temporality stemming out of the past there is also for Bergson a temporality which operates from the present towards the past. This Bergsonian duration is closer to Heidegger's when the latter says that the future proceeds towards the past.

**Globalization**

Globalization seems to be a rather general construct, an abstract conceptualization of thoughts to deal with general processes characterizing the dynamics of our common world at present and for the future. It is a fascinating concept covering the dynamics, systematicity of world inter change as well as the growing inter dependency of all continents and their respective societies, living standards, traditions, challenges and situations including the environmental and climate problems aggravating at the time. At the beginning of the 21st century, we are confronted with huge problems and opportunities, but a feeling of disorientation and cultural crisis in the air. All religions and ideologies have failed and broken down. Science is fragmented and traditional philosophies are reduced to mere commentaries of texts of the past. They are not in a position to provide an acceptable orientation to the increasingly well-informed, cosmopolitan and scientifically minded humans of our time. The need of the hour is to have a 'global philosophy' which is relevant for all of mankind and not just for the people of a particular culture or society. It has to be compatible with science and take into account the relevant results of science. According to Bertrand Russell, the contemplation of the cosmos "makes us citizens of the universe, not only of one walled city at war with all the rest. In this citizenship of the universe consists man's true freedom and his liberation from the thralldom of narrow hopes and fears ........".

Is the concept of 'Globalization' relevant to Bergson's Philosophy ? The answer is affirmative. The seeds of Globalization are to be found in the concept of 'open morality' which he advocates in his *The two sources of Morality and Religion*. Throughout his work, Bergson identifies habit with reason which can be narrowed down to 'closed' or 'constituted' reason. 'Closed Morality' belongs to the world of legislation and therefore social. The laws of 'Closed Morality' create nations based on race, culture, language, religion and ideologies. The laws of the states are imperatives and hypothetical in nature and are aimed at social preservation. The closed morality is restrictive and tends to dehumanize. It arises out of pressure from society and acts as a propulsive force whereas the open morality has the effect of an appeal. Closed value is something solidified and immanent in material reality. Open or true value is transcendent and creative. Closed morality is 'legal' whereas open morality is 'human'. A philosophy which is 'Global' must incorporate the essential characteristics of Bergson's 'Open Morality'. Since traditional political theories take the nation state as their frame work of reference the globalised problems of culture, science, fashion, finance and economics can not be resolved by adhering to the obligations of 'closed morality'. The large problems of over population, ecological crises, of war and peace, migrations and terrorism can not be solved at the national level. Bergson's 'open morality' which is truly 'human' and transcends the national and other narrow barriers can show the way in solving the Global problems. The underlying principle of Bergson's Élan Vital is to overcome the obstacles created by "matter" which are static. It functions at different levels and at each level it replaces the static with more fluid and dynamic principle which we can find in the Bergsonian opposites: Matter-Memory, Intellect-Intuition, Space-Time, Closed Morality—Open Morality. Whether the replacement of Newtonian Theory of space which is static by Einstern's theory of Relativity or the replacement of Closed Morality by Open Morality, there is continuous effort of the Élan Vital to over come the static. In the case of Globalisation too it replaces the ethics of closed society which we witness in the contemporary social, cultural political structures with more dynamic ethics of open morality.

## REFERENCES

1. James W. Felt, "Intuition, Event Atomism, and the self", Bergson and Modern Thought, Eds. A.C. Papanicotion and P.A.Y. Gunter New York and Paris: Harwood Academic Publications, 1987, p. 38.
2. Henri Bergson, *Time and Free Will*, p. 110.
3. Henri Bergson, *The Creative Mind*, (trans by M.L. Andison), New York: The Wisdom Library, 1946, p. 88.
4. *Ibid.*, p. 48
5. *Ibid.*, p. 74.
6. Lewes S . Fever, *Einsterin and the Generations of Science*, New York: Basic Books, 1974. Louis De Broghi, *"The Concepts of Modern Physics* and *Bergson's Ideas on Time and Motion"* in *Bergson* and *the Evolution of Physics*, Knoxvilli : University of Tennessee Press. 1969, pp. 45-62.
7. P.A.Y. Gunter, Review of Milic Capek's *Bergson and Modern Physics: A reinterpretation and Re-evaluation*, South Western Journal of Philosophy, Vol. 6, February 1975, p. 159.
8. *Ibid.*
9. P.A.Y. Gunter : Review of Jean Milet' s Bergson et le Calcul infinitesimal: Ou, La raison et le temps, *Journal of the History of Philosophy*, Vol. XIV, April 1976, Number 2, p. 244.
10. *Ibid.*, p. 245.
11. Bergson, *Creative Evolution*, pp. 218-219.
12. *Ibid.*, pp. 220-21.
13. P.A.Y. Gunter, "Bergson's theory of Matter and Modern

Cosmology", Journal of the History of Ideas, Vol. XXXII, October-December 1971 (U.S.A)

14. Bergson, *Creative Evolution*, p. 263.
15. *Ibid.*, p. 270, Cf. pp. 263-267.
16. *Ibid.*, p. 271.
17. For steady-state Cosmology: Herman Bondi, *Cosmology* (Cambridge, 1961); Fred Hoyle, Galaxies, *Nucbi and Quasars* (New York, 1965).
18. P.A.Y.Gunter, *op. cit.*, pp. 529-30. For an exposition of the basic suppositions of evolutionary Cosmology: Georges Lemaitre, The *Primeval Atom* (New York, 1950); George Gamow, *The Creation of the Universe* (New York, 1952).
19. Carl Gustav Jung, "The Content of the Psychoses, Part II, 1914" in Collected Papers on Analytical Psychology, edited by C.E. Long (London: Balliev, Tindall and Cox, 1922) p. 293.
20. P.A.Y. Gunter, "What Jung Learned from Bergson" (Unpublished Article).
21. C.G. Jung, Psychology of the Unconscious, p. 335.
22. *Ibid.*, p. 416.
23. Carl Gustav Jung, *"Instrict and the Unconscious" Contribution to Analytical Psychology*, p. 274.
24. *Ibid.*, p. 274.
25. *Ibid.*, p. 275.
26. C.G. Jung, "On some Crucial Points in Psycho analysis" in *Collected Papers on Analytical Psychology*, pp. 274-75.
27. *Ibid.*, p. 293.
28. C.G. Jung, "The Psychology of Dreams", in *Collected Papers on Analytical Psychology*, pp. 309-10.
29. C.G. Jung, Psychological Types, trans. By H. Godwin Baynes (New York: Har Court, Brace and Company, (1944) pp. 461-67, 508-13, 567-69.
30. Edmund Husserl, Phenomenology of Internal time Consciousness, Ed. Martin Heidegger, Trans. James S.Churchill Bloomington and London: Indiana University Press, 1971, pp. 157, 84.
31. Martin Heidegger, "The Concept of Time in the Science of History" Trans. Harry S. Taylor and Hans W. Uffelman Journal of the British Society for Phenomenology, Vol.9, No.1, January, 1978, pp. 5-6.
32. *Ibid.*

33. *Ibid.*, p. 6.
34. *Ibid.*, p. 8.
35. *Ibid.*, p. 4.
36. *Ibid.*, p. 8.
37. Martin Heidegger, *Being and Time*, Trans. John Macquarric and Edward Robinson, New York and Evanston, Harpe & Row Publishers, 1962, pp. 500-501.
38. Martin Heidegger, *The Basic Problems of Phenomenology*, Trans. Albert Hofstadter, Bloomington: Indiana University Press, 1982, p. 244.
39. Henri Bergson, *Time and Free Will*, pp. 157-58.

# Bibliography

**Works by Bergson**

1. *The and Free Will,* translated by F.L. Pogson (London : George Allen and Unwin Ltd., Ruskin House, 40, Museum street, W.C. 1. New York : The Macmillan Company, 1910).
2. *Matter and Memory,* translated by Nancy Margaret Paul and W. Scott Palmer (London : George Allen and Unwin Ltd., New York : The Macmillan Company, 1929).
3. *Laughter,* An Essay on the Meaning of the Comic (Le Rire, 1900) translated by Cloudesley Brereton and Fred Rothwell (Macmillan and Co. Ltd., St. Martin's Street, London, 1921).
4. *An Introduction to Metaphysics,* translated by T.E. Hulme (Macmillan and Co. Ltd., St. Martin's Street, London, 1913).
5. *Creative Evolution,* translated by Arthur Mitchell (Macmillan and Co. Ltd., St. Martin's Street, London, 1920).
6. *Mind-Energy,* Lectures and Essays translated by H. Wildon Carr (Macmillan and Co. Ltd., St. Martin's Street, London, 1920).
7. *The two Sources of Morality and Religion,* translated by R. Ashley Audra and Cloudesley Brereton (Macmillan, 1935).
8. *The Creative Mind,* translated by Mabelle L. Andison (New York : Philosophical Library, 1946).

**Other Books**


9. Bernard, C. : *Introduction a l' etude de la medecine* experimentale (1865).
10. Berthelot, R. : *Un Romantisme utilitaire.*
11. Binet and Fere : *Animal Magnetisme*
12. Biran, Maine de : Oeuvres (Tisserand)
13. Carr, Wildon H. : (i) *The Philosophy of Change* (Macmillan, 1914).

    (ii) *The Scientific approach to Philosophy* (Macmillan, 1924).
14. Cournot, A.A. : (i) *Essai sur les fondaments de nos connaissances* (1851) Vol. I. (ii) *Traite de l' enchainement des idees fondamentales dans les sciences et les arts* (1861), Vol. I.
15. Donson, G.R. : *Bergson and the Modern Spirit,* (London, 5 Essere Street, Strand, W.C. 1914).
16. Driesch, H. : *The History and Theory of Vitalism.*
17. Durkheim, Emile : *Elementary Forms of the Religious Life.*
18. Durant, Will : *Outlines of Philosophy Plato to Russell* (London, Ernest Been Limited, 1962).
19. Edwin, Irwin (Editor) : *The Philosophy of Schopenhauer* (The Modern Library, N.Y : 1928).
20. Fichte, J.G. : *The Vocation of Man.*
21. Flewelling, Ralph Tyler : *Bergson and Personal Realism* (The Abingdon Press, New York, 1920).
22. Fouillee, A. :

    (i) La Liberte et le determinisme

    (ii) L'Evolutionisme des idees—forces

    (iii) La Psychologie des idees—forces.
23. Guyan, A. :

    (i) La Philosophie etla sociologie d' Alfred Fouilee.

    (ii) *La Genese*

    *(iii) Esquisse d'une morale sans obligation ni sanction.*
24. Gunn, Alexander J : *Bergson and his Philosophy* (Methuen and Co. Ltd., 36 Essex Street, W.C. London, 1920).

25. Hartmann, von : *Philosophy of the Unconscious.*
26. Hegel, G.W. :
    *(i) System der Philosophie*
    *(ii) Phenomenology* (translated by Baillie)
    *(iii) Philosophy of Religion* (translated by Speirs and Sanderson).
27. Hermann, E. : *Eucken and Bergson, their significance for Christian Thought* (London, James Clarke and Co., 13 and 14 Fleet Street, 1912).
28. Hoffding, Harold : *Modern Philosophers and Lectures on Bergson* (Macmillan and Co. Ltd., St. Martin's Street, London, 1915).
29. James, William :
    (i) *The Varieties of Religious Experience* (Collier Books, New York, 1961).
    (ii) *A Pluralistic Universe* (Longmans, Green and Co., Fourth Avenue and 30th Street, N.Y., 1916).
30. Joad, C.E.M. : *Introduction to Modern Philosophy* (London : The University Press, Oxford, 1958).
31. Kann, A. : *Henri Bergson und meine Ideen.*
32. Lachelier, J. : *Psychologie et metaphysique,* Oeuvres, I.
33. Lalande, A. : *La Dissolution oppossee al evolution.*
34. Lindsay, A.D. : *The Philosophy of Bergson* (J.M. Dent and Sons Ltd., Bedford Street, Strand, W.C., 1911).
35. Lotze, H. : *Metaphysic.*
36. A.A. : *Bergson's Doctrine of Intuition* (London : Society for promoting Christian knowledge, New York and Toronto: The Macmillan Co., 1922).
37. Maitra, S.K. : *The Meeting of the East and the West in Sri Aurobindo's Philosophy* (Sri Aurobindo Ashram, Pondicherry, 1956).
38. Montague, Pepperell Wm : *Great Visions of Philosophy, Varieties of Speculative Thought in the West from the Greeks to Bergson* (The open Court publishing Company, Illinois, 1950).

39. Otto, Rudolph : *Mysticism East and West* (Collier Books, New York, 1962).
40. Rao, Lakshmana Ayyagiri : *Metaphysical Psychology of Henri Bergson* (Andhra University Press and Publications, Waltair, 1971).
41. Ravaisson, J. : *Rapport sur la philosophie en France au XIX me siecle* (ed. of 1885).
42. Renouvier, C. : *Essais de Critique generale Premier essai* (1954).
43. Ribot, T. :
    *(i) English Psychology*
    *(ii) L' Heredite psychologie*
    *(iii) Diseases of the Memory*
    *(iv) Les Maladies de la personnalite*
44. Ruhe, Algot and Paul, Nancy Margaret : Henri Bergson, An account of his life and Philosophy (Macmillan and Co. Ltd., St. Martin's Street, London, 1914).
45. Russell, Bertrand :
    (i) *Mysticism and Logic and other Essays* (Longmans, Green and Co., 39, Paternoster Row, London, E.C. 4, 1925).
    (ii) *Our Knowledge of the External World* (George Allen and Unwin Ltd., Ruskin House, 40, Museum Street, London).
46. Santayana, George :
    (i) *Winds of Doctrine* (London, J.M. Dent and Sons, 1926).
    (ii) Reason in Religion (Collier Books, New York, 1962).
47. Schopenhauer : *The World as Will and Idea.*
48. Smith, Colin : *Contemporary French Philosophy* (London, Methuen and Co. Ltd., 11, New Fetter Lane E.C. 4, 1964).
49. Spencer, Herbert : *The Principles of Psychology.*
50. Stallknecht, Newton P. : Studies in the Philosophy of Creation with especial reference to Bergson and Whitehead (Princepton, Princeton University Press, 1934).

51. Stephen, Karin : *The Misuse of Mind,* (London : Kegan Paul, Trench, Trubner and Co. Ltd., New York : Harcourt, BRace and Company, Inc., 1922).
52. Suzukum, D.T. : *Mysticism Christian and Buddhist* (Collier Books, New York, 1962).
53. Tannery, J. : *Science et philosophie.*
54. Ulrici, H. : *Compendium der Logik.*
55. Weisenburg and Mc Bride, K.E. : *Aphasia.*
56. William, John Mac : *Criticism of the Philosophy of Bergson* 38, George Street : T and T Clark : Edinburgh, 1928).

**Journals**

1. Benda, J. : *Dryssen, Bergson und die deutsche Romantik,* Revue de Paris CXII (May 15, 1915), 187. C.
2. Bergson : "De la simulation inconsciente dans l' hypnotisme", *Revue philosophique,* XXII (1886), p. 525.
3. Corrance, Henri C. : "Bergson's Philosophy and the Idea of God," *The Hibbert Journal,* Vol. 12 (1913-1914), p. 374.
4. Dumesnil, G. : "La Sophistique contemporaine", *Amitee de France,* 1912.
5. Flowelling, Ralph Tyler : "Bergson and Personalism", *The Personalist,* Vol. XIV, 1933, p. 89.
6. Gunter, Pete A.Y. :

   (i) "Biological time and biological development", *Bilingual journal,* No. 1, Fall 1971, *Lecomte Du Nouy Association* (H.Q. : 15, Avenue Elisee Reclus 75—(Paris (7e) France.

   (ii) "Whitehead, Bergson, Freud : Suggestions toward a Theory of Laughter" ? *The Southern Journal of Philosophy* (U.S.A.), Vol. 4, Summer, 1966, No. 2.

   (iii) Review of Milic Capek's *Bergson and Modern Physics, Southwestern Journal of Philosophy* (U.S.A.), Vol. 6, No. 1, February, 1975.

   (iv) "Bergson's Reflective Anti-Intellectualism", *The Personalist,* Vol. 47, No. 1, Winter, 1966, published by the

School of Philosophy, University of Southern California, U.S.A.

(v) "Biological Time and Biological Mechanism : Reflections on the 'New Embryology'," The Southwestern Journal of Philosophy, Vol. II, Numbers 1 and 2.

(vi) "The Heuristic Force of Creative Evolution", *The Southwestern Journal of Philosophy* (U.S.A.), Fall 1970, Vol. I, No. 3.

(vii) "Bergson's Theory of Matter and Modern Cosmology", *Journal of the History of Ideas*, Vol. XXXII, No. 4 (U.S.A.), October-December, 1971.

(viii) Review of *Bergson et le calcul infinitesimal : ou, La raison et le temps*. By Jean Millet (Paris : Presses Universitaires de France, 1974, pp. 184.

7. Lenon, P. : Critical Review of Bergson's *Less deux sources de la Morale et de la Religion—Mind*, Vol. 41 (1932), p. 490.
8. Lovejoy, A.O. : "Some Antecedents of the Philosophy of Bergson", *Mind*, Vol. XXII (1913) pp. 465-483.
9. Maitra, S.K. : Third article on "The Philosophy of Henri Bergson", published in *Review of Philosophy and Religion*, Vol. 11, January, 1942.
10. Marin, F. : "Sur l'origine des especes", *Revue scientifique*, 4th series, XVI (1901), p. 580.
11. Mukherjee, Radha Kamal : "Religious Experience", *The Sociological Review*, April 1930, and Roots of Religion, Social Forces, Vol. VIII, p. 10.
12. Parkes, H.B. : "The Tendencies of Bergsonism", Scrutiny, A quarterly Review, Vol. IV, No. 1, 1935, published by the Cambridge University Press (London : Bentley House, 200, Euston Road), p. 423.
13. Ravaisson, J. : "De l' habitude", *Revue de metaphysique et de morale*, XII (1894), p. 10, 16, 28, 34.
14. *Mind*, Vol. XXI, N.S., p. 39.
15. *Scientia*, Vol. XXI, 1917.

# Index